P9-CST-353

Redefining
Black Film

Redefining Black Film

Mark A. Reid

UNIVERSITY OF CALIFORNIA PRESS

Berkeley / Los Angeles / Oxford

University of California Press
Berkeley and Los Angeles, California

University of California Press
Oxford, England

Copyright © 1993 by The Regents of the University of California

Library of Congress Cataloging-in-Publication Data
Reid, Mark (Mark A.)
    Redefining Black film / Mark A. Reid.
      p.   cm.
    Includes bibliographical references and index.
    ISBN 0-520-07901-9 (cloth).—ISBN 0-520-07902-7 (paper)
    1. Afro-Americans in the motion picture industry.
    2. Afro-Americans in motion pictures. I. Title.
PN1995.9.N4R45 1993
791.43′089′96073—dc20   92-6458
                                           CIP

Printed in the United States of America

1 2 3 4 5 6 7 8 9

The paper used in this publication meets the minimum requirements of American National Standard for Information Sciences—Permanence of Paper for Printed Library Materials, ANSI Z39.48-1984 ♾

For Sylvie

Contents

Acknowledgments

Many people have helped to bring this book to fruition. The late Darwin T. Turner guided my thoughts on black film through our sometimes contradictory debates surrounding black identity, gender issues, and class consciousness. During my graduate work at the University of Iowa, I benefited from the mentoring of professors Turner and Jonathan Walton, and my colleagues in the African American World Studies Program created an atmosphere in which critical debates on the constitution of black culture and experience were numerous. It was in this fertile soil of Iowan cornfields and black scholarship that I began to write the first version of *Redefining Black Film.* Ernest Callenbach sustained Turner's initial support and read several versions of the manuscript until it became the book it now is.

The writing of this book required the same support as the making of a film: well-wishers, financial backers, and a production crew. Sergio Alexandro Mims, Steve Look, John Williams, and others were constant sources of information on upcoming films produced by black filmmakers. In the early period of my research, Carolyn Calloway-Thomas, Jim Naremore, Phyllis Klotman, Gloria Gibson-Hudson, Frances Stubbs, and Indiana University's Black Film Archive provided me with a singular opportunity to view rare black-oriented films and to teach my first black film class. During this same period, two French critics of film, Guy Hennebelle and Janine Euvrard invited me to edit *Le Cinema Noir Americain,* a project that placed me in contact with an international group of film critics. This book reflects my collaboration with European,

American, and African writers who are interested in the development of a critical approach for the study of black-oriented film.

Shorter versions of chapters one, three, four, and six have appeared in *Black Film Review, Jump Cut, Film History,* and *Black American Literature Forum,* respectively. I would like to thank the editors of these journals, David Nicholson, Richard Koszarski, Julia Lesage, John Hess, Chuck Kleinhans, and Valerie Smith, who helped to shape my thinking on African-American film. I would also like to thank the anonymous readers at University of California Press who further scrutinized my thoughts and David Leverenz and Sylvie E. Blum, who corrected my "imperfect cinema" approach to writing about black film. Together, the editors and readers strengthened my prose and forced me to rethink certain aspects of my argument. I especially would like to thank Sylvie for reading several versions of the manuscript and David for editing the final draft. The Museum of Modern Art and stills archivist Terry Geesken assisted in the selection of most of the stills and Women Make Movies, a distributor of independently produced women's films, provided the stills in chapter six.

Outside of the academy, my parents, relatives, and friends on both sides of the Atlantic kept me aware of *lived* experiences that should not escape any theoretical analysis of the plurality of voices within black and world cultures.

Finally, I want to express my gratitude to the University of Florida's Division of Sponsored Research and its Center for African Studies, the Florida Endowment Fund's McKnight Junior Faculty Program, and the government of Burkina Faso for financial support that enabled me to visit film archives in the United States, Europe, and West Africa.

Introduction

Redefining Black Film describes two interrelated histories: that of black independent film production and that of black participation as writers and directors in three different genres of black-oriented films controlled by whites. Even when commercial films are made by black writers and directors, a black perspective that acknowledges differences of race, class, gender, and sexuality rarely surfaces. Therefore, a history of black film must employ critical tools that speak to these differences and do not concentrate only on one of these issues. I also argue that the history of African-American film must include a discussion of black independent films. In this book, I show how black independent film differs from black commercial film and argue that the two forms must not be discussed as though they were identical. Many earlier books that document this area define black film too broadly and presume that any film with black characters is a black film. Other works identify black film as those works written or directed by blacks, and some texts use subjective criteria such as aesthetics or a black perspective to define black film. I find that these faulty or limited definitions do not describe the formal aspects of black film.

Film books that discuss African-American films use critical approaches that emphasize white-directed, -written, and -produced films about black America. For example, the black-image approach has generated almost three decades of black-oriented film books: Peter Noble's *The Negro in Film* (1948), V. J. Jerome's *The Negro in Hollywood Films* (1950), Edward Mapp's *Blacks in American Films* (1971), James Murray's *To Find an Image* (1973), Lindsay Patterson's *Black Films and Film-Makers* (1975), Donald Bogle's *Toms, Coons, Mulattoes, Mammies, and Bucks* (1973), and, to a lesser extent, Daniel J. Leab's *From Sambo to Superspade* (1975) and Thomas Cripps's *Black Film as Genre* (1978).

In contrast, this book presumes that American film criticism must be augmented and corrected by descriptions and analyses of films produced by black people and of filmmaking in which black people controlled the key creative aspects of production. Present and future film histories must emphasize the innovations of black filmmakers and black screenwriters as well as discern the difference between black commercial filmmaking and black independent filmmaking.

This book *uncovers* the black film history that other critics and historians, inadvertently or by design, have helped to bury by selectively focusing on major studios and their films about, but not by, blacks. These interpretive histories, like the films they discuss, perpetuate dominant assumptions by avoiding serious historical issues and ignoring the polyphonic forms of black subjectivity. I want to disrupt the prevailing approach to the study of blacks in American film by providing critical analysis of a more than seventy-year-old film practice.

In distinguishing black commercial film from black independent film, I establish my own definition of "black independent film": a film that focuses on the black community and is written, directed, produced, and distributed by individuals who have some ancestral link to black Africa. I describe the rejuvenation of black independent film that resulted from the 1960s civil rights movement, the emergence of black consciousness, the War on Poverty programs, and the resurgence of feminism in black cultural production. All of these forces broadened the opportunities for black participation in the film and television industries.

By discussing specific examples of three major film forms—comedy, urban action, and black family films—I show how major studio-distributed black films present tendentious images of blacks, especially black women. (The term tendentious refers to images that objectify and ridicule blacks for the benefit of a viewer or listener.) I argue that this tendentious quality also occurs in films such as Melvin Van Peebles's *Sweet Sweetback's Baadasssss Song* (1971) and Spike Lee's *She's Gotta Have It* (1986), which are performed, written, directed, and produced by African-Americans. Thus, a valid examination of black film must separate the black commercial film from the black independent film in order to examine what types of films blacks create when they retain control over the distribution of their films.

Film histories that fail to distinguish black commercial films from black independent films tend to focus entirely on the commercial films. Consequently, they bury black film history by analyzing it according to "relevant" theoretical criteria that are not applicable to black independent film. They also do not consider the particular cultural experiences of African-Americans. Other well-meaning critics analyze black-oriented films according to the popular Marxist, feminist, and psychoanalytic approaches that appeal to the widest reading audience—white male and female middle-class intellectuals. This hegemonic critical triumvirate attempts to subsume—that is, colonize—black film scholarship under the aegis of one of the three critical stances. Such appropriation of black film history and theory minimizes the importance of racial difference as a valid critical approach and, thereby, implies an imaginary America in which problems related to race are less important than those related to class or gender. I do, however, argue for a gender-class-race analysis that also examines black film in relation to its political and cultural context in African-American history. Therefore, my critical approach will engage a feminist-Marxist-black cultural reading of African-American film production and reception.

"Race" and "Gender" as Functions of Ideology

Feminists have developed theories of spectatorship that engender Marxism with a gynocentric notion of ideology. Using Louis Althusser's Marxist analysis of ideology, Teresa de Lauretis indicates the shortsightedness of orthodox Marxism:

> When Althusser wrote that ideology represents "not the system of the real relations which govern the existence of individuals, but the imaginary relation of those individuals to the real relations in which they live" and which govern their existence, he was also describing, to my mind exactly, the functioning of gender.[1]

An engendered space is negotiated within Althusserian Marxism, one of the most humanistic branches of Marxist thought. Here, *negotiation* describes the process of including a formerly excluded concern. For example, conventional Marxism does not consider gender concerns to be as important as those of class affiliation. Therefore, Marxist feminists must negotiate for the inclusion of gender (an engendered space) within conventional Marxism. One such feminist is de Lauretis, who is aware that her feminist entreaty will receive a cold welcome from orthodox Marxists. She rebuts their imagined discourse: "But, it will be objected, it is reductive or overly simplistic to equate gender with ideology. Certainly Althusser does not do that, nor does traditional Marxist thought, where gender is a somewhat marginal issue, one limited to 'the woman question.' "[2]

Traditional Marxism argues that there is a constant struggle between the owners of production and the workers they employ. Such Marxists should welcome those who desire to incorporate feminism and race as functions of ideology. The women's movement has sought to articulate a feminist approach to the practices of Marxism. People of color have introduced theories that include "race" in the debate over the function of ideology in Marxist, Freudian, and feminist circles. Marxist and Freudian approaches recognize the relevance of gender, but continue to deny the importance of race in their theoretical practices. Surely, a race-class-gender analysis would provide Marxism and psychoanalysis with a more inventive analytical strategy than the reigning dualism. A few critics have pursued such work while borrowing insight from the Marxist debates on questions of gender and ideology.[3] To this end, Teresa de Lauretis gives an engendered reading of the function of ideology in Althusser:

> Reading on in Althusser, one finds the emphatic statement "All ideology has the function (which defines it) of 'constituting' concrete individuals as subjects." If I substitute gender for ideology, the statement still works, but with a slight shift of the terms: Gender has the function (which defines it) of constituting concrete individuals as men and women.[4]

I propose that *race* functions to constitute concrete individuals as white and black. Here the movement from subjects to men and women, to black and white, not only "marks the conceptual distance between two orders of discourse, the discourse of philosophy or political theory and the discourse of 'reality,' " it marks the conceptual distance of race and the race-oriented forms of popular culture.[5] In this construction, race informs a progressive Marxism that previously integrated only class- and women-centered theories of spectatorship and postulated an engendered, yet raceless subjectivity.

For the purposes of clarity, the black commercial film is limited here to any feature-length fiction film whose central focus is the Afro-American community. This film is written, directed, or produced by at least one black person in collaboration with non-black people. Films included in this category are distributed by major American film companies.

The black independent film is defined as any feature-length fiction film whose central focus is the Afro-American community. Such films are written, directed, and produced by Afro-Americans and people of African ancestry who reside in the United States. These films are not distributed by major American film companies.

I use the phrase "black mode of artistic production" to identify a filmmaking process in which blacks have written, directed, and produced their films without financial control by major American commercial film producers, distributors, or exhibitors. The phrase does not describe or evaluate the films' aesthetic representation of African-American life or ideology.

During the period covered in this book, 1900–1990, the major commercial distributors, include the post-1930 Micheaux Film Corporation, Allied Artists, American International (AIP), Atlas Films, Avco-Embassy Pictures (Embassy), Columbia Pictures (Columbia), Cinema 5, Cinemation Industries (Cinemation), Cinerama Releasing Corporation (Cinerama), Fanfare Films, Hammer Brothers, Island Pictures, Metro–Goldwyn Mayer (MGM), National General Pictures (NGP), New World Pictures (NWP), Paramount Studios (Paramount), Samuel Goldwyn, Jr., Twentieth Century–Fox (Fox), United Artists (UA), Universal Pictures (Universal), and Warner Brothers (Warner).

The first chapter presents the earliest practitioners of black-controlled independent filmmaking and focuses on their work in comedy, family melodrama, and action films. This chapter provides a framework to discuss black-oriented film genres in later chapters on African-American comedy, black family film, and black action film.

The African-American comedy film genre comprises black-oriented fiction films whose casts include popular black comedians and whose primary purpose is to amuse its interracial audiences through the use of hybrid minstrelsy and social satire. The comedy may employ the elements of sex and violence, but these elements are not vehicles to create or alleviate the audience's anxieties.

The black family film genre is a black-oriented fiction film whose action takes place within a typical black family whose narrative function and ideological aim is the restoration of the family. Thus, if the narrative of a family film uses humor, it is only to develop themes and issues of secondary importance to the reestablishment of the family circle. For example, *Gone Are the Days* (Hammer, 1963) and *Five on the Black Handside* (UA, 1973) both feature black family units, but the former is a black comedy film because its narrative primarily generates the comic form of satire, and the latter film is a family film whose comic elements function to ameliorate and unify the family rather than (as in *Gone Are the Days*) to criticize racism.

The black action genre includes black-oriented feature-length fiction films whose narratives may use a combination of the following elements: sexually explicit scenes, physically or psychologically aggressive acts that result in violence, and fearful or horrifying characters or events. These elements usually limit protagonists to mythic or superhuman roles. This genre includes various subtypes like the horror film, the Western, and the gangster-detective film. This book, however, limits analysis to urban action films because they can present controversial themes and provoke violent urban funk. One needs only to recall the violence that occurred outside film screenings of John Singleton's *Boyz N the Hood* (Columbia, 1991). Chapters five, six, and seven critically assess how recent black filmmakers and their films simulate certain forms of black "reality" while they avoid dramatizations of sexism, homophobia, and classism within the black community.

Chapter five provides an ideological analysis of Spike Lee's three independently produced, studio-distributed urban black comedies and his failure to create empowered black female characters. Chapter six moves from the issues of race and black masculinity to a discussion of these issues within a black feminist context.

A contribution to nascent black feminist theory of film production and audience reception, chapter six presents an Afrocentric feminist interpretation of two aspects of black independent filmmaking. The chapter includes a description of black womanist film production and possible forms of its reception. This black feminist reading is a two-fold form of resistance to a raceless feminism and a phallocentric pan-Africanism. To provide an example of black feminist perspective, I analyze three black-oriented films made by women who have a racial connection to black Africa.

The seventh chapter returns to my initial focus on the late 1960s and early 1970s. I describe that period's renaissance in independent black filmmaking and critically assess the films of a few African-American men who employ a black feminist perspective. Throughout this book, and particularly in chapters six and seven, I argue that socioeconomic factors and sociopsychic desires conjoin and pressure black writers and directors to avoid portraying controversial topics. Consequently, few studio-distributed films portray interracial intimacy as meaningful and successful. Black women are passive victims or wanton waifs, and black gays and lesbians are ridiculed in films that depict them as members of the black community.

1

Early African-American
Film Companies

Foster Photoplay Company's
Black Comedies

In 1910, Bill Foster (also known as Juli Jones) founded the Foster Photoplay Company in Chicago.[1] Bill Foster was the first African-American to establish a film production company. Foster has been described as: "A clever hustler from Chicago, he had been a press agent for the [Bert] Williams and [George] Walker revues and the [Bob] Cole and [Billy] Johnson's [comedy-musical] *A Trip to Coontown* [1898], a sportswriter for the [Chicago] *Defender,* an occasional actor under the name of Juli Jones, and finally a purveyor of sheet music and Haitian coffee."[2] *A Trip to Coontown* "was a musical with a plot—one that completely broke with the minstrel tradition and told a story through music, song and dance."[3] Thus, by 1910, Bill Foster had had access to the innovative style of the black comedians and musicians who worked in the theater. It was the black theater that influenced Foster's development of the black-oriented, comedy film.[4]

Foster's first productions were the black-cast comedy shorts *The Railroad Porter* (1912) and *The Fall Guy* (1913). *The Railroad Porter* premiered at Chicago's white-owned and black-managed Grand Theatre in July 1913, and had its New York premiere at the Lafayette Theatre in September. The *New York Age,* a black weekly, described Foster's two films as "comedy films representing Negro life without putting the race in a ridiculous light." His films presented a variety of respectable African-American characters. Nevertheless, film historian Daniel J.

Leab disagrees with the *Age*'s appraisal: "*The Railroad Porter* . . . was a comedy that does not seem to have been very different in style and content from the films depicting blacks that were turned out by the industry."[5] Thomas Cripps states that the film was an "imitation of Keystone comic chases completed perhaps three years before [D. W. Griffith's] *The Birth of a Nation* [1915]."[6] Both historians seem to ignore an important narrative element of *The Railroad Porter* which Keystone, Chaplin, and other contemporaries of Foster tend to ignore—that black characters can not only be porters for whites but also waiters in respectable black cafés in middle-class African-American communities. The *New York Age* of September 25, 1913, states that the film

> dealt with a young wife who, thinking her husband had gone out on "his run," invited a fashionably dressed chap, who was a waiter at one of the colored cafés on State Street, to dine. However, the husband did not go out, and, upon returning home found wifey sitting at the table serving the waiter all the delicacies of the season. Mr. Husband proceeds to get his revolver, which he uses carelessly, running the unwelcome visitor back to his home. Then the waiter gets his revolver and returns the compliment. . . . no one is hurt . . . and all ends happily.

In this synopsis one discovers that: there is a married woman who can afford to invite another person to eat with her; this married woman desires the company of a "fashionably dressed chap"; the chap is employed as a waiter as opposed to being unemployed; there existed black cafés on State Street in Chicago's black neighborhood in 1912; and neither "Mr. Husband" nor the "fashionably dressed chap" uses his revolver to harm the other. It is true that *The Railroad Porter* has a comic chase scene as Cripps has said, but Foster's use of the comic chase is far different from the stereotypical chase of the petty black thief in the Rastus Series: "The very titles of popular favorites like *How Rastus Got His Turkey* and *Rastus in Zululand* [1909 and 1910] suggest the type of low comedy of the split-reelers."[7] Leab is correct in implying that *The Railroad Porter* is similar to the comedies turned out by the industry. Nevertheless, Foster photoplays altered the popular Rastus stereotype by using African-American sociocultural realities as the content of his films. Some of these realities are the existence of a black middle-class, employed northern blacks, and blacks who patronize black-owned restaurants.

In 1914 the Foster Photoplay Company toured the South with their comedy shorts *The Railroad Porter* and *The Fall Guy,* the detective film *The Butler* (1913), and the melodrama *The Grafter and the Maid* (1913). The company's star, Lottie Grady, formerly of Chicago's Pekin Theatre stock company,[8] sang while the projectionist changed the reels. Thus,

Foster's film program retained some of the technique of vaudeville roadshows, yet broke with the "coon" tradition established by Thomas Alva Edison's *Ten Pickaninnies* (1904) and *The Wooing and Wedding of a Coon* (1905) as well as Sigmund Lubin's Sambo and Rastus series (1909, 1910, and 1911).[9] Aiming at a black audience, Foster needed to create comedy that would appeal to the widest segment of his audience. Foster's films introduced a black perspective for a black audience who desired images different from the Euro-American comedies of the industry.

Lincoln Motion Picture's Black Family Films

The Lincoln Motion Picture Company, founded in Los Angeles, California, in 1916, was probably the second black film company established in the United States. Lincoln was started by a group of black Los Angeles citizens. Noble Johnson, a bit actor at Universal Studios, was Lincoln's president, director-scenarist, and leading actor from 1916 to 1918. Clarence Brooks doubled as the Lincoln's second leading actor and company secretary. Other founding members of the company included Dr. James Thomas Smith, who was the vice-president and treasurer, Willes O. Tyler, the attorney, and Dudley A. Brooks, the company's assistant secretary. In 1918, George Perry Johnson, Noble's brother, became Lincoln's general booking manager. Harry Gant, a Universal Studios cameraman, was the only white who was affiliated with Lincoln.

Their productions, like those of the Foster Photoplay Company, deliberately used a black slant because Lincoln agreed with Foster that "blacks should make movies with black performers for black audiences. . . . that there was a market waiting for such films and that the black entrepreneur would profit financially."[10] Lincoln produced films demonstrating the concept of American individualism. The company's films, unlike Foster's comedies, were serious narratives with plots constructed around a black, rural hero's realization of some admirable ambition. Lincoln Motion Picture Company, although confined to three shorts and two feature-length films, produced mostly family-oriented pictures.

The company's first two-reeler was *The Realization of a Negro's Ambition* (1916).[11] The film's black protagonist, James Burton, is a Tuskegee graduate who leaves his father's farm and his girlfriend. Burton's departure allows him to seek his fortune out West on the California oil fields. When he arrives in California, Burton is denied an oil drilling job because he is black. The denial of an opportunity to work for the oil company becomes his major conflict. Nevertheless, Burton surmounts this obstacle by saving the life of a wealthy, white oilman's daughter and is rewarded with a job from her father. Later, the owner discovers that Burton has a degree in civil engineering and makes Burton the head of an oil expedition. Through a series of discoveries, Burton realizes that the geological features of his father's farm resemble those of the California oil fields. He returns home, becomes wealthy through his discovery of oil, and weds his hometown sweetheart.

This short synopsis reveals what I consider to be the major elements of the black, rural family film. A hero whose family includes a mother and father and who lives in a rural, non-industrial environment. The narrative limits the use of humor, sex, and violence that is found in the black comedy and action film genres. Despite its conventional plot, *Realization* presents a serious portrayal of a middle-class African-American family.

According to the October 14, 1916, edition of the black Los Angeles weekly the *California Eagle,* Lincoln's second two-reeler, *The Trooper of Company K* (1916), told the "simple story of a good-for-nothing fellow who joins the army and finds himself all man with a big heart and good enough for a little girl who is [at] home waiting for him." The *Eagle* emphasized the film's importance as a historical documentary of the June 1916 "Carrizal Incident." The incident occurred during the Mexican-American War's Carrizal battle, when Troops K and C of the all African-American Tenth Calvary almost perished. The newspaper account noted that the film "will rank as an exceptional picture if only for its historical value, commemorating as it does the battle at Carrizal, where our boys made such a good fight against overwhelming odds, sacrificing their blood and life for their country." The narrative develops a rural, unkempt, and lazy character named Jimmy Warner (also known as "Shiftless Joe"). Warner joins the army and becomes part of Company K of the black Tenth Calvary. During the battle at Carrizal, Warner rescues his injured captain and is decorated with honors. After his high school sweetheart reads of Warner's courageous deeds, she accepts him as an appropriate suitor. The plot shows the hero's development from a shiftless character into a man who rises to meet a challenge, succeeds honorably, and returns home to marry his true love. The protagonist in *Trooper* is a redeemed black hero; he presents an alternative image both to the "coon," a shiftless black stereotype, and to the "Tom," a black who, when faced with racism, resigns himself to an inferior place.

In creating the black, rural family film genre, Lincoln established a new type of black protagonist, a middle-class hero who believes in the puritan work ethic. The actor who played the rural hero in both of Lincoln's films was the already popular Noble Johnson, "one of the most active and highly paid black movie actors." He had an athletic build and a light complexion,[12] attributes that were central to Lincoln's image of a black rural hero. The athletic build gave the hero the appearance of strength. The choice of an actor with a light complexion corresponded to contemporary black theatrical conventions that gave the more important roles to fair-skinned African-American actors.

At this point in African-American film history, the black family genre's hero closely resembled roles played by the white actor Douglas Fairbanks. Both Fairbanks and Noble usually performed roles that emphasized their athletic physiques and espoused the values of hard work and self-esteem. When the popular black writer Oscar Micheaux began to produce films in 1919, he continued the practice of using a light-complexioned hero, but he placed his hero in an urban environment. Micheaux adapted his second novel, *The Homesteader* (1917), for the screen in 1919. The first African-American to produce a feature-length film, Micheaux created characters that were either in the process of migrating from the South to the North or were northern inhabitants of an urban ghetto.

Between 1913 and 1915 the one-reeler or two-reeler film, commonly called a short, had been replaced by the feature film, which became the main attraction in a movie program. As Lewis Jacobs writes, "the supply of feature film was swelled in 1913 by feature-length importations from Europe."[13] D. W. Griffith's *The Birth of a Nation* revealed that the American audience and film industry were ready for feature-length films—within a year, *Birth*'s return at the box office amounted to more than seven times its production costs.

Foster's one-reelers and Lincoln's two- and three-reelers were not of sufficient duration to compete with feature-length films. To retain their audience, black producers were forced to produce longer, better narratives. Thus, Micheaux's production of feature-length films was an important advance that enabled him to successfully compete with white independent producers of black-oriented films.

Oscar Micheaux and Black Action Films

In 1918 Oscar Micheaux founded the Micheaux Film and Book Company. His brother Swan Micheaux was Secretary-Treasurer and General Booking Manager, Charles Benson assisted Swan in the Chicago-based distribution and financial office while Tiffany Oliver and W. R. Crowell operated the Roanoke, Virginia office, and A. Odams, owner of the Beaumont, Texas, Verdun Theatre, controlled distribution in the southwest region.

Micheaux's action films, like other cultural productions of the Harlem Renaissance, were imaginative reflections of a proud, aggressive New

Negro whose new morality condoned retaliatory action against white racist aggressions. New cultural "objects" such as black action films were created for this new group of urbanized, race-conscious blacks who were learning to lessen their need for approval by white America. Blacks were becoming politically and culturally aware consumers, and the black market required products tailored to their new sensibilities.

To gain a popular black audience, Micheaux's action films presented the twenties from a black perspective. Whereas Lincoln Motion Picture productions were serious melodramas that espoused conventional middle-class puritanical ethics, Micheaux productions attracted audiences by dramatizing subjects that Lincoln films avoided. His films introduced black-oriented themes like interracial intimacy, lynching, passing, and other controversial subjects such as urban graft, wife beating, gambling, rape, and prostitution to their audience. For example, Micheaux's *The Homesteader* focuses on a black man who falls in love with a white woman. Perhaps for the first time in an American film, a sexual relationship between a black man and a white woman was not portrayed as the rape of the white woman. Thus, *The Homesteader* gave black audiences a favorable image to combat D. W. Griffith's image of "pure black bucks," which Donald Bogle described as, "big baadddd [sic] niggers, over-sexed and savage, violent and frenzied as they lust for white flesh."14

According to film curator Pearl Bowser, "Micheaux financed his . . . film [*The Homesteader*] in the same way he had financed the publication of the book [*The Conquest* (1913)]—by selling shares in his Western Book and Supply Co. to the white farmers. . . . He raised $15,000 to produce *The Homesteader,* the first feature-length [8 reels] independent black production."15 His profits from *The Homesteader* provided him with enough money to produce his second feature, *Within Our Gates* (1920).

Within Our Gates includes a horrifying dramatization of an African-American man being lynched. Micheaux himself had witnessed the anti-Semitic lynching of Leo Frank in Atlanta, Georgia.16 The court convicted Frank, a Jewish white man, for the murder of a white, southern Christian woman. Because *Within Our Gates* portrayed racial lynching, a topic that Hollywood refused to dramatize until after World War II, it should be the starting point of any discussion of the cinematic treatment of lynching. The film depicted the lynching of a black sharecropper, Jasper Landry, accused of murdering his employer, a white plantation owner. The portrait of a proud, landowning, black man contrasted sharply with the image of envious white men who considered Jasper Landry an uppity black. The film so graphically presented the lynching that a racially-mixed censorship board fought against its Chicago screening.17

Micheaux's next film was the eight-reeler *The Gunsaulus Mystery* (1921) whose plot reintroduced the theme of racial lynching. Together, *Within Our Gates* and *The Gunsaulus Mystery* portray two of the most virulent forms of hatred—anti-Semitism and racism against blacks. Micheaux's vanguard cinematic portrayals of racial lynching need to be considered in any social history of American film. In particular, his sensitivity to the shared horror of racism and anti-Semitism should be noted. A similar dramatic borrowing occurred in Carl Foreman's 1949 screen adaptation of Arthur Laurents's 1948 Broadway play *Home of the Brave.* Laurents's play depicted anti-Semitism but Foreman's screen adaptation dramatized anti-black hatred.

Micheaux's third feature, *The Brute* (1920), presented steamy love scenes and portraits of urban lowlifes in black dives and gambling joints. The topics of wife abuse and racial lynching were dramatized in a setting of social decadence. *The Brute* portrays the married life of a black underworld figure, Bull Magee, who beats his wife Mildred, a widow who has remarried. Ultimately, Mildred's first husband returns, and Bull Magee is defeated. The film's second plot focused on black boxer Sam Langford, a prize fighter who struggled against lynching.

Despite the moral worthiness of the film's two topics, self-conscious black critics denounced the "scenes of crap games, black dives, wife-beating, and women congregating to gamble" for portraying the New Negro as less than human. According to the *New York Age*'s entertainment critic Lester Walton, these scenes were not pleasing to blacks who desired positive images of the African-American community.[18] In contrast, the white men who headed local censor boards deplored the aggressive images of blacks, which they thought would incite blacks to riot. In Chicago, the censor board rejected the film because it feared that interracial violence on the screen might rekindle the racial tensions of Chicago's July 1919 race riot.[19] Despite the opposition by some blacks and whites, the film was well received by the black masses. This fact demonstrates that popular black tastes sometimes differ from the tastes of black and white critics who want to define aesthetic standards.

The Symbol of the Unconquered (1920)[20] dramatized a black man's struggle to retain ownership of valuable oil lands in the face of Ku Klux Klan attempts to chase him off. In addition to showing the terrorist tactics of the KKK, the film also portrayed a romance between the black man and a black woman who was initially mistaken for white. Thus, the film depicted a supposed interracial romance as well as the theme of passing.[21] The 12 December 1920 *New York Age* stated that this picture "is regarded as most timely, in view of the present attempt to organize night riders in this country for the express purpose of holding back the advancement of the Negro." On 1 January 1921, the *New York Age* stated that *Symbol* "graphically shows up the evils of the Ku Klux Klan. The biggest moments . . . are when the night riders are annihilated . . . by a colored man with bricks."

Even though *Symbol,* like *The Realization of a Negro's Ambition,* is set in the American West, the films differ in their picture of black life in that section of the country. Unlike Lincoln Motion Picture's *Realization,* a family film that portrayed a black man who patiently endured racism and obtained the right to prospect oil by saving a white oilman's daughter, Micheaux's action film shows that the black protagonist must physically battle against the violence of racism to retain his oil-rich land. The difference between the two suggests that *Symbol* reflects a turning point in African-American thought. Instead of emphasizing the long-suffering virtues of black Americans, Micheaux felt his black audiences would accept violence, urban lowlifes, interracial intimacy, and steamy love scenes.

Micheaux's reading of the African-American moviegoer anticipated by fifty years the commercial black-oriented films of the early 1970s. Moreover, the "colored man with bricks" who defeats the Klan is a superhero, an ancestor of such heroes of the 1970s as Sweetback, who appears in Melvin Van Peebles's *Sweet Sweetback's Baadasssss Song* (1971). The protagonist's retaliatory violence toward the Klan in *Symbol of the Unconquered* becomes an essential requirement of the seventies black action-film protagonists. The formula also dictated that the protagonist be sexually appealing to the opposite sex. Together, these requirements generated narratives that tend to exploit violence and explore black sensuality while the film depicts racist acts perpetrated by white villains. Micheaux's action films were forerunners of these 1970s film types, and for much the same reason: Micheaux's choice of controversial subjects and selection of black-oriented themes are evidence of an entrepreneur whose first goal is to make a profit and then, if popular tastes would allow, to present positive images of African-American life.

Micheaux's place within the Harlem Renaissance is exemplified in his choice of dramatic themes. His portrayal of black urban life, which included gangsters, sexually liberated women, and self-assertive blacks, reflected a community of cosmopolitan blacks. He pioneered the development of the black action film genre. Like the post–World War II years of black political activism, exemplified by NAACP legal briefs against racial discrimination and the work of A. Philip Randolph, the post–World War I years brought about sociopsychical changes in the African-American community, including Marcus Garvey's black nationalist form of capitalism (circa 1916) and Alain Locke's aesthetic philosophy, which guided Micheaux and other black artists during the Harlem Renaissance.

The Decline of the Indies

Despite the early pioneering efforts of the Foster Photoplay Company, the Lincoln Motion Picture Company, and the Micheaux Book and Film Company, black independent filmmaking was almost nonexistent by the late 1920s. Several developments in the American film industry stopped black independent filmmakers from reaching a black audience. The attraction of Hollywood, which momentarily opened its doors to black entertainers in the twenties, drew the best-known black stars away from black independent filmmakers. For example, even though Evelyn Preer made her film debut in Micheaux's *The Homesteader* and continued as a featured actress in most of his productions, she left Micheaux to work in films by white directors: "She expressed great admiration for Micheaux but maintained that 'colored actors would get their best chances from white directors'."[22] In 1928 Preer appeared in an Al Christie comedy short, *Melancholy Dame* (Paramount), which portrayed "Negro 'high society' in Birmingham," Alabama.[23] Preer was featured in other Christie spoofs of the black middle-class. In 1930 she received star billing in Harry Gant's black-oriented musical *Georgia Rose* (Aristo).[24] Preer finally escaped such black-cast films in Josef von Sternberg's *Blonde Venus* (Paramount, 1932), a Marlene Dietrich vehicle in which Preer played a very minor role along with Jean Harlow, Lena Horne, and Hattie McDaniel.[25] Perhaps these white-directed films did not offer Preer her "best chance," but they did produce paychecks during the Depression.

The pattern of Preer's film career was not unusual for black artists of that period, many of whom began by working in black-cast films and later found employment in major film studio productions. For example, Clarence Brooks, who first appeared in Lincoln Motion Picture's *Realization,* later starred as Doctor Marchand in *Arrowsmith* (Paramount, 1931). Paul Robeson made his film debut in Micheaux's *Body and Soul* (1924) and then was lured into productions by white studios.

The economic effects of the Great Depression forced many black performers to seek opportunities in Hollywood. They thought that financial opportunities would be better there than in the films of black producers. A basis for such optimism can be found in two 1930 California *Eagle* articles. One article observed that "as a casual example of what the motion picture industry [Hollywood] means to Los Angeles Negro citizens by way of employment and its effect upon their economic situation, one studio paid $2,307 to colored extras last week."[26] By the year's end, the *Eagle* reported that motion picture employment during the month of October had benefited the black Los Angeles community of actors and actresses.[27] In 1931, however, the *Eagle* article finally admitted the detrimental effects of the Depression on black producers, music composers, and singers who were "hard hit" by the Depression.[28] Thus, it is understandable that during the Depression many African-American entertainers sought employment in Hollywood.

It is equally understandable why major studios employed a few talented black singers, dancers, and comedians throughout the years of the Depression. Writing in 1929, a critic observed, "It is significant that with the coming of talkies, the first all-Negro feature pictures were attempted by the big companies. White America has always made much of the fact that all Negroes can sing and dance. . . . it is supposed to get particular pleasure out of the Negro's dialect, his queer colloquialisms, and his quaint sense of humor. . . . With the talkie, the Negro is at his best."[29] Moreover, Hollywood welcomed black entertainers because the black voice seemed particularly suited for the new talkies. By 1940, even white independent producers of low-budget, black-oriented films were threatened by Hollywood, which continued to attract well-known black stars. For example, Ted Toddy's independent Million Dollar Pictures produced *The Duke Is Tops* (1938), which featured Lena Horne in her film debut. A few years later, Horne signed a long-term contract with Metro–Goldwyn Mayer.[30] Horne's MGM contract was the mixed result of NAACP pressure and the United States government's effort to create a national consensus, which included a new policy on race relations. The government asked Hollywood to promote racial liberalism in its productions. Black performers continued to seek opportunities in Hollywood as long as studios sought to hire them.

Black film producers declined not only because their stars went to Hollywood, but also because of the Depression and the cost of sound and camera equipment. Moreover, whites consolidated their control of distribution markets and forced black producers into unequal partnerships. Micheaux was among those whose film company's suffered, and he filed for bankruptcy in February 1928. His operational problems resulted from faulty distribution systems, censorship rulings, print costs, the high cost of sound technology, and the centralized management of Harlem theaters. These factors forced Micheaux into an interracial alliance with Harlem theater owners Leo Brecher and Frank Schiffman.[31]

After the 1929 reorganization of the Micheaux Film Corporation, he continued to make films but his productions were collaborative interracial efforts—black creative talent backed up by white financing. In 1931 the *New York Age* reported, "While Mr. Micheaux remains the titular head of the motion picture company, the control has passed into the hands of the lessees of the Lafayette and other theaters in Harlem."[32] Thus the Micheaux films produced after his company's 1929 re-incorporation cannot be considered black independent films, according to my definition, because black independent films must be produced by black-controlled film production companies.

Little is known about how long Micheaux remained with the owners of Harlem's theaters but the effects of this partnership created new directions in black film production. Micheaux's 1929 move to black commercial film, as opposed to black independent film, signaled a pause in African-American independent film production. The pause would last nearly forty years.

"After 1931," Thomas Cripps writes, "blacks raised capital from Frank Schiffman of Harlem's Apollo Theatre, Robert Levy of Reol, and white Southern distributors like Ted Toddy and Alfred Sack. By the end of the decade, the Goldberg brothers, Arthur Dreifuss, Edgar G. Ulmer, Arthur Hoerle, Emmanuel Glucksman, Harry and Leo Popkin, Robert Savini, Ben Rinaldo, and Jed Buell, all white, prevailed."[33] If Cripps is indeed right to say "all white prevailed," then film historians and critics have been mistaken in calling Micheaux's post-1930 films "black independent cinema." In fact, Micheaux's post-1930 work more than likely anticipated two decades of black-directed, white-financed, low-budget, commercial films made outside of Hollywood. By the late fifties, Hollywood major studios would adopt the low-budget, black commercial film in an effort to compete with television.

To recapitulate the history I am tracing here, Foster was the first significant African-American producer of black independent cinema— that is, any film focused on the black community and written, directed, and controlled by blacks in collaboration with either non-black technical crews or predominantly black crews. Foster's *The Railroad Porter* introduced the black comedy-film genre, which I define as any black-oriented, commercial or independent black film aimed to entertain its audience through the use of comic formulae. In the comic film genre, the Foster Photoplay Company competed directly with white companies such as Sigmund Lubin, who produced coon comedies for the much larger and financially attractive white market. As feature-length film production improved, Foster's comedy shorts lost their popularity and in 1916 he stopped making independent black comedy shorts.

When Lincoln Motion Picture Company's *The Realization of a Negro's Ambition* appeared, it marked the beginning of a second genre, the black family film. The plots included in this genre take place within a recognizable black family situation, and most of this company's films avoid presentations of violence, sex, and crime. The company introduced the first filmic representation of rural black heroism, a theme that no longer appealed to audiences after World War I.

At this point, Micheaux productions developed the black action film genre with plots that treated controversial themes that white Hollywood and black Lincoln had ignored. His productions altered black film history by introducing feature-length format and the explicit treatment of interracial marriage, lynching, passing, black criminality, and black sexuality.

In 1929, even though Micheaux retained his name in the Micheaux Film Corporation, the corporation was financed and controlled by two whites. Thus, Micheaux Corporation films do not represent black independent filmmaking.[34] *A Daughter of the Congo* (1930) and *The Exile* (1931) are transitional in African-American film history: the first film marks the beginning of Micheaux's collaboration with Quality Amusement, a large, white firm; and the latter film is the first all-talkie, feature-length, black commercial film. This interracial collaboration captured the Harlem film market and gave Micheaux access to other black film houses: in Philadelphia, the Dunbar; in Washington, D.C., the Howard; in Baltimore, the Colonial; and in Norfolk, the Attucks.

The Schiffman-Brecher-Micheaux union presaged later interracial collaborations in Hollywood: Louis Peterson's co-scenario *Take a Giant Step* (United Artists, 1959); Lorraine Hansberry's *A Raisin in the Sun* (Columbia, 1961); Melvin Van Peebles's *Sweet Sweetback's Baadasssss Song* (Cinemation);[35] Sidney Poitier's direction of three black screenplays for Warner Brothers (*Uptown Saturday Night, Let's Do It Again,* and *A Piece of the Action* in 1974, 1975, and 1977, respectively); and, more recently, Spike Lee's writing, directing, and acting in *She's Gotta Have It* (Island Pictures, 1986), *School Daze* (Columbia, 1988), and *Do the Right Thing* (Universal, 1989). All of these enterprises recall the way in which Micheaux relied on the Quality Amusement Corporation's film distribution circuit.

2

African-American Comedy Film

African-American comedy film describes any comedy whose narrative is focused on the black American community. This chapter and those that follow analyze the mediation between textual, sociopsychic, and socio-economic phenomena. My analysis focuses on the production and reception of subtypes of African-American comedy, family, and action film.

In order to understand how African-American film comedy was shaped between the 1960s and 1980s, one must understand traditional elements of popular American race humor. The terms "blackface minstrelsy," "hybrid minstrelsy," and "satiric hybrid minstrelsy" refer to the most pervasive subtypes of African-American comedy film.

Blackface Minstrelsy Processes of Production and Reception

Blackface minstrelsy is an early popular form of American race humor. Even the denotation "blackface" emphasizes the importance of race in the construction of this comic form. Yet, noting the denotative racial quality—a black mask or an African-American presence—will not reveal the cultural codes of reception nor the social history of this form. White actors such as Edwin P. Christy and Ben Cotton helped to create blackface minstrelsy. The minstrel comics objectified African-American oral traditions, physiognomy, dress, dance, and song.[1] By masquerading in blackface, whites objectified African-American life experiences. From the viewpoint of an assimilative gaze, blackface minstrelsy allows whites to take pleasure in the "hostile or sexual aggressiveness" of blacks while the white race escapes the harm that such dramas assign to the African-American community.

The constructive properties of blackface minstrelsy include an addresser, an imaginary "black" object of ridicule, and an interested spectator. These three properties make blackface minstrelsy similar in textual construction to the tendentious joke. Both forms require an addresser, an object of ridicule, and a viewer-listener.[2] In a tendentious joke, the ridiculed object has a similar function as African-Americans in blackface minstrel humor and women in pornography, since blacks and women are objectified for the pleasure of whites in one instance and men in the other instance. Before the 1960s, minstrel comedy on the radio depended primarily on the "blackened" voices of Freeman Gosden and Charles Correll, two white men. They created a blackened form of radio humor that made its transition to film and, later, to television.

The "Amos 'n' Andy" radio show was created in 1928 by Gosden and Correll, who spoke in a black dialect and performed the roles of Amos Jones and Andy Hogg Brown, respectively. Their fifteen-minute WMAQ radio show was originally broadcast in Chicago. As of August 19, 1929, it was nationally aired for six nights weekly from 6:00 to 6:15 P.M. eastern standard time. The program's prime-time radio slot gave the series an opportunity to attract a family audience. When the radio program was limited to Chicago, it presented a series of sketches that focused on two aspiring black men who had migrated from Georgia to Chicago; later, when the program was nationally broadcast, their place of migration was changed to New York's Harlem.

"By 1930," according to Arnold Shankman, "the program was more popular than any other show on the air, and its two [white] stars were the highest paid performers on radio."[3] The program's popularity illustrates the appeal of white-created black dialect humor that was similar to minstrel shows. In discussing the effect that sound technology had on the revival of minstrelsy, Thomas Cripps writes, "The coming of sound brought a revival of the minstrel show, that most racist form of entertainment, on film. The success of Amos 'n' Andy's radio show undoubtedly . . . [contributed] strongly to the trend."[4]

To gain popularity, Gosden and Correll used minstrel caricatures and avoided any portrayal of the socioeconomic effects of unemployment, segregated housing, and inadequate health care in African-American communities. Perhaps these defects were the reasons why black scholar Benjamin Brawley, African Methodist Episcopalian bishop W. J. Walls, and the Pittsburgh *Courier* publisher Robert Vann as well as the NAACP attempted, without success, to stop the radio broadcast of the "Amos 'n' Andy" program. During the latter part of 1930 and spurred by pressures from the black middle class, the three black leaders began their campaign against the radio show.

Some African-Americans, however, were willing to overlook these caricatures because the radio program presented blacks who embodied basic American virtues—such as the desire for self-betterment, the pursuit of economic independence, and undaunted optimism in the face of failure. The radio show presented northern blacks as optimistic supporters of these American middle-class values at a crucial time—during the Depression and World War II. For example, in an effort to become self-employed, Amos and Andy purchase an automobile and establish the Fresh Air Taxicab Company; this attempt at private enterprise reflected a desire to participate in the American dream by becoming entrepreneurs. One critic wrote, "The dominant themes of the series were completely consistent with . . . bourgeois aspirations. The search for work and the dreams of success dominated Amos 'n' Andy for over thirty years. The various schemes pursued by the pair and their friends to achieve status and prestige, to enter the stolid middle classes, was totally attuned to the Dream."[5]

Thus, the radio program spoke to certain audiences in both the black and the white middle classes. This articulation of American values may explain why some members of the black community and a few of their newspapers, such as the Chicago *Defender* and the Gary *American,* were reluctant to boycott the sponsor of the radio program and, later, would become avid fans of the television show.[6]

An especially interesting element of the analysis of the black spectator or listener of racially tendentious comedy is that audience's ability to find humor in a racist discourse that, one might assume, requires an equally racist audience positioning. But reception is not constructed so simply. Audiences have the ability to overlook the obvious racism and seize the humane properties of the overtly racist discourse. In this viewing or listening position, the racist discourse receives oppositional readings by an internally persuasive discourse

> which is more akin to retelling a text in one's own words, with one's own accents, gestures, modifications. Human coming-to-consciousness, in Bakhtin's view, is a constant struggle between these two types of discourse: an attempt to assimilate more into one's own system, and the simultaneous freeing of one's own discourse from the authoritative word, or from previous earlier persuasive words that have ceased to mean.[7]

Relying on the popularity of the radio show, Correll and Gosden starred in an Amos 'n' Andy film in 1930. This film, *Check and Double Check* (Radio-Keith-Orpheum), used white men in burnt-cork makeup

From Check and Double Check. *Courtesy of the Museum of Modern Art Film Stills Archive.*

to perform the major black roles. Emphasizing the same caricatures that typified minstrel shows, white men spoke the black dialect of the stage and overdressed for their professional roles or dressed shabbily for their roles as laborers. Fortunately, the film failed at the box office.

The box office failure of *Check and Double Check* may have lessened the widespread use of burnt-cork caricatures in filmed dramatizations of black life. *Check and Double Check* did not adequately represent the visual image of an urban black community which black and white spectators had expected, and white men appearing in burnt-cork displeased many blacks and whites who enjoyed the "Amos 'n' Andy" radio show.[8] The visual rejection of burnt-cork white performers parallels the auditory rejection of certain silent film performers whose voices displeased their audience. Audiences rejected many of them because there was some kind of dissonance between image and voice.[9] Similarly, when the "Amos 'n' Andy" radio show made its transition to television, a more naturalistic standard prevailed and concordance between racial image and racial voice was expected. Consequently, black entertainers were hired to perform the roles that had been previously performed by the two white men who had created the radio program. This transition fostered the hybrid minstrel comedy subtype, which is discussed below. The popularity of black-oriented comedy on television began with the "Amos 'n' Andy" prime-time CBS situation comedy series, which began on June 28, 1951. CBS produced eighty-one half-hour segments until June 11, 1953. Later, CBS syndicated this situation comedy until it was pulled from distribution in 1966.[10]

The three modes of transmission (radio, film, and television) and the sociohistorical period created a set of conditions for blackface minstrel humor. Mainstream filmgoers rejected the images of two white men in blackface, although this audience had accepted the radio broadcast of their minstrel voices. The rejection of blackface reflects the ambivalent nature of minstrel comedy, which resists repetition but is confined to a racist narrative form. The transition from auditory semblance to its appearance as a visual reality, required black performers to "naturalize" modern blackface minstrelsy and resulted in a hybrid form. Black performers were caught in a pact with the pressures of repetition and invention.

Hybrid Minstrelsy and Black Employment as Comic Types

The term hybrid minstrelsy describes a second style of black-oriented humor. This comic type borrows some of its aural and visual qualities—such as burnt-cork makeup, malapropisms, shabby dress, and coon and mammy caricatures—from white-oriented minstrel humor.[11] For example, at the turn of the century Bert Williams, a light-skinned black used burnt-cork, dressed in threadbare clothes, and, though he spoke impeccable English in private life, used malapropisms in his stage roles.

This hybrid humor resulted from the fact that black and white writers as well as black performers concentrated on satisfying the expectations of white audiences, which demanded a non-threatening African-American humor. "A public humor perpetuated by outsiders uses a minority group, Negroes, as the brunt of half-truth caricatures. . . . Perhaps one of the appeals of this image is that it evoked an image of a romanticized Southern tradition [or a wishful fantasy, during the sixties civil rights era and thereafter] . . . in which [blacks] were believed to be happy and contented in their subservient roles in American society."[12] Black actors supported this form because it provided much-needed employment.

Some stereotypical elements that characterized both the radio series and the film remained in the black-cast televised version of "Amos 'n' Andy." For example, the television series included many male characters who resembled derogatory stereotypes from the minstrel shows:

Andrew (Andy) Hogg Brown, the obese, domineering, and lazy partner of Amos; George (Kingfish) Stevens, a scheming, well-dressed con man and president of a black fraternal organization; and Lightnin', a slow-moving janitor. These men reflect some elements of the coon stereotype as Donald Bogle defines it: "no-account niggers, those unreliable, . . . lazy, . . . good for nothing more than . . . butchering the English language." This minstrel caricature is found also in Sapphire Stevens, a modernized version of a domineering mammy, who is constantly criticizing the inadequacies of her husband George. Partly because of the show's continued use of these caricatures, some members of the African-American community began to actively oppose the airing of the television series.[13]

From its radio beginnings through its short career in Hollywood and its transition to television, "Amos 'n' Andy" spanned nearly forty years on American broadcast media. The series focused on the Northern black middle-class. The show suggested that this group possessed some American economic values and aspirations, but it severely undercut this positive image by using minstrel humor to ridicule the group.

Because the studio system had declined and television became the major source of entertainment by the mid-fifties, the popular tastes of the television audience determined the continued production and syndication of certain images.[14] The longevity of the "Amos 'n' Andy" television show demonstrates how black performers made a previously racist humor appeal to a new generation of consumers. The cross-racial popularity of the show suggests that an audience can select between two types of discourses—one can either accept the authoritative discourse, or appropriate and create an internally persuasive discourse. Thus, the industry exploited the function of black presence in minstrel comedy to minimize criticism against its racially tendentious product. Spectators could view hybrid minstrel comedy without moral compunction since the images inferred the acquiescence of the objectified racial other.

Criticism directed at black minstrel performers for their participation in such films is misguided. Black actors had little power over the production of hybrid minstrel works and their presence in these films does not reflect racial self-hatred. Rather, critical analysis should examine how socioeconomic forces determine where and when blacks participate in American popular culture. Analysis must not ignore the socioeconomic and sociopsychic factors that determine any relationship between the oppressed and the oppressor nor dismiss the sociopsychic strategies that maintain the humanity of those oppressed. In describing the need of an enlightened society to hide smut under the veil of a joke, Freud writes, "Only when we rise to a society of a more refined education do the formal conditions for jokes play a part. The smut [racism] becomes a joke and is only tolerated when it has the character of a [black] joke. The technical method which it usually employs is the allusion—that is, replacement by something small, something remotely connected, which the hearer reconstructs in his imagination into a complete and straight-forward obscenity [racism]."[15]

This technical method is also used in narratives in which black performers denigrate the black community. A Marxist interpretation of this phenomenon would describe the black performer as a dupe whose performance is solely determined by economic factors. One cannot deny the power of money and its ability to sustain the relationship between black performer and racist narrative. But one should not overlook the need to explain how sociopsychic factors create ruptures in the economy and produce the indeterminate nature of spectatorship. Therefore, any comedy or racist narrative form must contend with the transitory desires of an audience. Racial and gendered audiences can and do permit oppositional readings of the reception of hybrid minstrelsy and thereby maintain their humanity. Yet psychological analysis never adequately describes the socioeconomic determinants that produce racist and sexist jokes. Interpretation must also incorporate the sociopsychic and socioeconomic factors that determine the popularity of a given film narrative.

When blacks such as Bert Williams performed in blackface minstrels, they rarely created a non-racist form. In comparison to white performers in blackface, the presence of black performers neutralizes the racist imagery in hybrid minstrelsy. Black presence validates the joke, veils the smut, and recycles it for a modern "enlightened" audience. Comedy is a psychic and economic expenditure with benefits for the producers, the performer-object, and the spectator. For example, the African-American actor Stepin Fetchit (Lincoln Theodore Perry) became a millionaire by performing coonlike caricatures. The interrelationship of economic production, psychic desires, and consumptive practices permitted Fetchit to repeat his hybrid minstrel caricatures. Stepin Fetchit never controlled a single aspect of film production. Regardless of his stated intentions, Stepin Fetchit's performances were determined by the contemporary socioeconomic and sociopsychic forces of his time.

In the production and reception of minstrel and hybrid minstrel comedies, whites can produce racial myths, believe myths that support their imagined racial superiority, or feel maligned by the production of these myths and create an oppositional form of reception. But a black performer such as Stepin Fetchit is permitted only the last two of these choices, both of which require black spectators to use oppositional strategies of reception. When a comedy film objectifies blacks, it produces both pleasure and pain for both racial groups but such feelings are not of the same quality and, therefore, must be differentiated.

Some theorists would have us believe that objectified individuals, through performance, become members of a hegemonic class. The rise of a black middle-class, or the appearance of black millionaire-comedians, however, does not imply the group's or the individual's general acceptance in American society. Stepin Fetchit's wealth would not ward off a possible lynching if he, during the period of his wealth and popularity, had accompanied his white wife to the South. This can also be said of Eddie Murphy, who received a racial slur from a woman working on *Coming to America,* a film he produced and starred in.

Black biographical studies should discuss issues of wealth and popularity as well as the performer's function in the film narrative, in film reception, and as a private citizen. The theoretical importance of the black comic lies in a film's successes *and* failures. An analysis of the popularity or unpopularity of certain black comedies might reveal change in the function of canonical narratives, the assimilation or appropriation of its authoritative discourse, and the inventive or repetitious nature of the product and performer.

Like its blackface counterpart, hybrid minstrelsy, in its most conventional form, shares the tendentious joke's triple process of narrative production. In the 1970s, the production of this subtype required black directors and screenwriters whose presence, like the black minstrel performer in blackface, enabled the naturalization, validation, and repetition of minstrelsy in a postmodern age. Examples of the reconstitution of the objectified blackened other appear in the black-directed and -written films *Cotton Comes to Harlem* and *Uptown Saturday Night.*

Hybrid Minstrel Film

In African-American comedy film, as in any creative project, invention is the result of the conjunction of socioeconomic forces and mythopoetic structures. American race humor comprises three forms of minstrelsy—blackface minstrelsy performed by whites and blacks, and hybrid and satiric minstrelsy performed exclusively by blacks. Hybrid minstrelsy, the second structure, is an oppositional strategy that adopts the internally persuasive discourse of blackface minstrelsy and its racially tendentious structure.

During the 1970s, many of the black comedians who had appeared on television variety shows or in sitcoms were featured in African-American comedy films. The first financially successful, hybrid minstrel comedy produced by a major studio was *Cotton Comes to Harlem* (United Artists, 1970).[16] *Cotton* was directed and cowritten by Ossie Davis, an African-American; the screenplay was adapted from a detective novel of the same title written by Chester Himes, an expatriate black novelist. Godfrey

From Cotton Comes to Harlem. *Courtesy of the Museum of Modern Art Film Stills Archive.*

Cambridge and Raymond St. Jacques, a dramatic actor, performed the roles of police detectives "Grave Digger Jones" and "Coffin Ed Johnson," respectively. These two Harlem detectives uncovered a crooked back-to-Africa scheme that had been organized by a black preacher.

Cotton belongs to the hybrid minstrelsy subtype of African-American comedy film.[17] Redd Foxx performs the role of "Uncle Bud," a junk man who resembles the shuffling janitor "Lightning" of the "Amos 'n' Andy" television show. Calvin Lockhart plays "Reverend Deke O'Malley," a womanizing con man who steals $87,000 from his congregation's back-to-Africa fund; the character "Deke" is modeled on George "King-fish" Stevens, whose schemes exploit members of his lodge. In addition, *Cotton* presents a ridiculous image of both the black church and its desire for African repatriation. This film is an example of the intellectual and artistic shortcomings of many of the African-American comedy films.[18] However, from a film industry standpoint, *Cotton*'s box-office success helped further the production of hybrid minstrel comedy film. *Cotton* grossed $5,200,000 but cost only $1,200,000 to produce.[19] The financial success of this film seemed to prove that a low-budget, hybrid minstrel film could attract a mainstream audience.

Uptown Saturday Night (Warner, 1974), the first major African-American comedy film directed and produced by Sidney Poitier,[20] utilizes techniques that had proved popular in *Cotton Comes to Harlem.* In *Uptown Saturday Night,* Bill Cosby costars in a comic role while Poitier performs a more dramatic role; this pairing is similar to the roles of Godfrey Cambridge and Raymond St. Jacques in *Cotton.* Similarly, *Uptown* also includes roles that portray the criminal elements in the black community. For example, Harry Belafonte and Calvin Lockhart, two matinee idols, are featured in the roles of crime bosses "Geechie Dan Beauford" and "Silky Slim," respectively. Furthermore, *Uptown* has elements of hybrid minstrel comedy. Flip Wilson's character presents a black preacher as a bantering fool. Another popular black comedian, Richard Pryor, appears in a role that makes a mockery of black detectives.

The film tells the story of Steve Jackson (Poitier) and Wardell Franklin (Cosby) who are caught in a holdup in an after-hours night club. When the robbers steal Jackson's wallet, which has a lottery ticket worth $50,000, he and Franklin get the help of rival gang leaders Geechie Dan and Silky Slim to retrieve Jackson's lottery ticket.

Like *Cotton, Uptown* avoids socioeconomic and sociopsychic subject matter because hybrid minstrel humor necessarily lacks any significant dramatization of African-American life. Accurate comic portrayal of such would require some emphasis upon the political purposes of African-American humor—"a psychological leverage . . . and . . . a weapon for survival against the harsh treatment" by oppressors of African-American people.[21] Instead, Poitier tried to ensure his film's popularity with a mainstream audience. For example, he used makeup and direction to turn "Geechie Dan Beauford" into a blatant comic imitation of Marlon Brando as "The Godfather" in the highly popular 1972 film of the same title. Poitier succeeded in gaining the popularity that he desired. Within a year, the film had earned about $6,650,000 in domestic rentals (the portion of box-office receipts that is returned to the distributor), more than *Cotton*'s domestic rentals. The popularity of both *Cotton* and *Uptown* reflects the pastiche quality of hybrid minstrel films insofar as they mimic a dead humor without a social or political intent. Fredric Jameson writes,

> Pastiche is . . . the imitation of a peculiar or unique style, the wearing of a stylistic mask, speech in a dead language: but it is a neutral practice of such mimicry, without parody's ulterior motive [like the ulterior motive of · satiric hybrid minstrelsy] without the satirical impulse, without laughter, without that still latent feeling that there exists something normal compared to which what is being imitated is rather comic. Pastiche is black parody that has lost its sense of humor.[22]

From Uptown Saturday Night. *Courtesy of the Museum of Modern Art Film Stills Archive.*

In *Let's Do It Again* (Warner, 1975), a sequel directed by Poitier, written by Richard Wesley, and produced by First Artists, Poitier repeated his popular formula. Once again Poitier and Cosby played major roles with Calvin Lockhart and John Amos as gangsters representing the required criminal elements. *Let's Do It* also benefited from a music score by Curtis Mayfield, who was popular with black and white audiences. The film reveals some hybrid minstrel elements including a plot that might have been conceived for the "Amos 'n' Andy Show." It tells of the scheme of two Atlanta working-class men. Clyde Williams (Poitier) and Billy Foster (Cosby) try to raise money for the construction of a new fraternal lodge. Bootney Farnsworth (Jimmie Walker) is transformed from a coward into a fierce middle-weight prize-fighter thanks to the hypnotic powers of Williams. Foster and Williams bet $20,000 at five to one odds with Kansas City Mack (Amos) and Biggie Smalls (Lockhart), two rival gamblers. When Farnsworth wins, the two lodge mem-

From Let's Do It Again. *Courtesy of the Museum of Modern Art Film Stills Archive.*

bers return to Atlanta with $100,000, which finances the construction of their new lodge. Later, Kansas City Mack discovers the hypnotic scheme and forces Williams to use his hypnotic powers on Farnsworth so that Farnsworth will lose the rematch. But the lodge brothers, assisted by their wives, again outwit the gangsters by betting that both fighters will be knocked out and by using hypnotism to ensure the result.

Let's Do It grossed fifteen million dollars and was *Variety*'s "Top Grossing" film for three weeks in December 1975. The financial success and crossover (interracial audience) appeal of *Uptown* and *Let's Do It* encouraged studios to continue to produce African-American comedy films. For example, in 1976, Universal produced *Car Wash*, a film about the life and experiences of black laborers in an interracial carwash business located in a black community.[23] Black comedians Franklyn Ajaye and Antonio Fargas appear in comedy roles while Ivan Dixon's and Bill Duke's roles explore serious social issues.

From Let's Do It Again. *Courtesy of the Museum of Modern Art Film Stills Archive.*

Cameo appearances by Richard Pryor in the role of "Daddy Rich," a well-dressed preacher, and the Pointer Sisters in the role of the "Wilson Sisters" provide the film with a sequence that resembles a variety show. In addition, the brief appearances of George Carlin and Professor Irwin Corey provide two instances of white comic relief in a basically African-American comedy film. These four cameo appearances function as vehicles to attract a larger mainstream audience. According to Michael Schultz, an African-American and director of *Car Wash*, the film's production costs were around $2 million and the film grossed about $12 million in domestic rentals.[24] The pastiche quality of this genre attracted more spectators than did the satiric hybrid minstrels, which also imitated blackface minstrelsy but tended to mock its source.[25]

The financial successes of *Cotton, Uptown, Let's Do It,* and *Car Wash* and their proven ability to attract and amuse mainstream audiences are a matter of record. But financial success and mainstream audience approval are not the most important criteria for determining the quality of an African-American comedy film. A focus on financial success and mainstream approval misses the underlying value of black humor and black film production. The traditional purpose of black humor has been to resist and subvert humor that ridicules members of the black community. Black

From Car Wash. *Courtesy of the Museum of Modern Art Film Stills Archive.*

humor is a humanized form of American ethnic humor. In this sense, traditional black humor is an oppositional discourse "which is more akin to retelling a text in one's own words. . . . Human coming-to-[black] consciousness . . . an attempt to assimilate more into one's own system, and the simultaneous freeing of one's own discourse from the authoritative word, or from previous earlier [black] persuasive words that have ceased to mean."[26] These four hybrid minstrel comedies, for the most part, do not portray experiences that are "derivative of the Negroes' unique social position."[27] However, as more African-Americans gained filmmaking and screenwriting skills, they attacked the canon of hybrid minstrel caricatures, and the African-American comedy film genre acquired a more contentious voice and politically diverse audience.

Like the transition of the "Amos 'n' Andy" radio show to television, blackface minstrelsy adapts to the socioeconomic and historical setting and, in time, transforms its racially objectified blackened other. This conversion permits a sort of "civilized" displacement of racism and produces a derivative form of blackface minstrelsy which I have referred to as hybrid minstrelsy. By the mid-1960s, however, the developing forces of black consciousness militated against overt exhibitions of hybrid minstrelsy. Though an assimilated hybrid minstrel style is present in the

1970s black-cast television comedies "Sanford and Son," "Good Times," and "The Jeffersons," it is more subtle because certain black protagonists simultaneously appropriated black power rhetoric while the narrative transmitted the opposite.[28] As the militant black consciousness movement vociferously criticized the overt minstrelsy, more attention was given to black humor that expressed social satire. This kind of humor characterized the work of such comedians as Dick Gregory and Godfrey Cambridge.

Hybrid minstrelsy is derived from the blackface minstrel tradition, a dominant form of Anglo-American humor. With the exception of the black performer in blackface, such as Bert Williams in comedy roles, hybrid minstrelsy assimilates, without negotiation, the malevolent character of blackface minstrelsy. However, neither spectators nor performers are determined by the racially tendentious hybrid minstrel film. They are determined by the strategies used to process and understand sociocultural objects.

There are three requirements for cultural communication: an addresser (the industry-artist) who must select codes to transmit, a chosen subject-object (the story and its elements), and an addressee (a spectator) who must use codes to interpret the message. Illustrative of the indeterminate nature of reception is the ongoing debate concerning the merits of "The Cosby Show," a televised, black-cast sitcom that portrays a black middle-class family called the Huxtables. The National Broadcasting Network and Bill Cosby (the industry-artist addressers) produce this black middle-class family sitcom (the chosen subject-object) for a cross-racial television audience (the addressee). The program is popular, attracts sponsors, and enjoys notoriety and economic success. The artist-producer, Cosby, receives a high salary. His salary enables him to sponsor an endowment for the black educational institution Spelman College (a subject-object). It also permits him to give a benefit performance for Jesse Jackson's 1988 presidential campaign (a subject-object). This is the socioeconomic importance of "The Cosby Show."

Equally important is the internal dialogue of the Huxtables, who are a civilized, loving, and middle-class black family (subject-object). The Huxtables project an image of a black successful family which is diametrically opposed to the economically successful and male-centered George Jefferson of the black family sitcom "The Jeffersons." George argues with his wife, berates his maid, distrusts his black laborers, and hates his white neighbors. Recognizing the shortsightedness that accompanies most televised images of ethnic life, can one deny that "The Cosby Show" advances some elements of the televised black family?

However, some critics view "The Cosby Show" as a white situation comedy in blackface. They argue that the show does not present the lived experiences of African-Americans. According to these critics, the typical black family is headed by a woman and is economically situated below the poverty line. These critics ignore both the determinism of the television medium and the indeterminancy of reception. Cross-racial reception is like the meeting of "two polyglots—one (the industry-artist) chooses the best language for speaking on a chosen subject (the African-American family sitcom), while the other (the interracial audience) begins the act of reception by establishing in which language, of those known to him, he is being addressed."[29] Critics who insist on the existence of a unique black family model ultimately "naturalize" that model, and repudiate other models as white imitations. These repudiations erase, through critical lynchings, those equally *lived* experiences of the "other" black people who become third parties in this critical debate.

According to Freudian psychoanalysis, the third party in the tendentious joke is an "inactive" spectator. A traditional Freudian-Marxist analysis of hybrid minstrelsy spectatorship would argue that socioeconomic and sociopsychic fears draw spectators to hybrid minstrel comedies. But viewing and listening can be a self-conscious strategy. It is not totally determined by socioeconomic factors. An actively engaged spectator never escapes the psychological effects of race and gender prejudices any more than Marxism escapes its fixation on economic issues. The process of spectatorship produces a network of relationships that are constantly in tension—race, gender, class, sexuality, and ethnicity. It is not a static relationship between the text—"The Cosby Show" or "The Jeffersons"—and a passive and unquestioning viewer. Any spectator may employ oppositional reading strategies to avoid the sexist and racist implications of a text. A hybrid minstrel spectator, then, is not an impassive reader who accepts the monologic narrative as it unfolds. It is possible for African-Americans (and others) to practice oppositional readings of hybrid minstrel comedies.

Satiric Hybrid Minstrelsy

A third element of African-American humor, satiric hybrid minstrelsy, was popularized during the civil rights movement by such African-American comedians as Jackie "Moms" Mabley, Dick Gregory, Godfrey Cambridge, and Flip Wilson. These comedians criticized racial and socioeconomic problems.[30] Like hybrid minstrelsy, this satiric component appealed to a white audience. But, unlike hybrid minstrelsy, satiric hybrid minstrelsy also appealed to a black audience who negotiated the contents and laughed with, and sometimes at, themselves as well as white Americans. Both whites and blacks tended to be entertained by the same jokes, which ridiculed contemporary racial and social inequities.

Satiric hybrid minstrelsy is a *negotiated* form of hybrid minstrelsy and shares the racially tendentious structure of the blackface and hybrid minstrel forms. In the satiric hybrid form, a racially objectified white (or any physically or psychically non-"black" person) becomes the target of "black" laughter. Thus, satiric hybrid minstrel films, such as the black-authored *Gone Are the Days* (Hammer, 1963) and *The Landlord* (UA, 1970), as well as the black-authored and -directed *Which Way Is Up?* (Universal, 1977) and *Hollywood Shuffle* (Goldwyn, 1987), sustain the racially tendentious structure of blackface minstrelsy.

The negotiated aspect of satiric hybrid minstrelsy requires that the black object become the subject of the narrative and the once objectified black be replaced by an equally objectified white (or any variation thereof).[31] Robert Downey's *Putney Swope* (Cinema 5, 1969) illustrates this racial reversal of subject-object positioning. The film portrays a predominantly white, Wall Street advertising firm whose board of directors includes one black, Putney Swope. During a board meeting to elect the next chairperson, the white members unknowingly elect Swope. He fires most of the white board members and creates a predominantly black board that includes a black woman. The firm adopts an urban black language style, namely black power rhetoric, and retains the capitalist motives and racist attitudes of the deposed white board members. Although this film was produced, written, and directed by whites, it exemplifies some characteristics of satiric hybrid minstrelsy—a focus on African-Americans, black socioeconomic empowerment, and the maintenance of capitalist and racist values. Thus, the mythopoetic experience of being the object of third-party pleasures is not a static relationship but one exhibiting external and internal dialogue.[32] In satiric hybridity, the objectified person or group may return a tendentious joke through the technique of "unification." This technique "lies at the bottom of jokes that can be described as 'ready repartees.' For repartee consists in the defense going to meet the aggression, in 'turning the tables on someone' or 'paying someone back in his own coin'—that is, in establishing an unexpected unity between attack and counter-attack."[33] Nevertheless, repartee maintains the racist conventions of minstrelsy and thereby celebrates racial essentialist notions. In the satiric hybrid minstrel film, the process of unification produces an *uninventive* rebellion, because the racial dualism that structures blackface and hybrid comedy equally determines the structure of satiric hybrid minstrelsy.

Satiric Hybrid Minstrel Film

In the late 1970s, certain African-American comedy films employed the technique of unification for the purposes of commenting on social issues. Although the creators of these films still wished to entertain and realize financial profit by appealing to the broadest American audience, the filmmakers also wished to present serious social issues that affected African-Americans and other racial minorities. After having directed financially successful hybrid minstrel films during the early 1970s, both Sidney Poitier and Michael Schultz, two African-Americans, pioneered in this new kind of comedy.

In 1977 Poitier directed *A Piece of the Action* (Warner), the third film in which he and Cosby costarred. The film was written by Charles Blackwell, an African-American, and the music was composed by Curtis Mayfield, another African-American. This film's action is focused on Manny Durrell (Poitier) and Dave Anderson (Cosby), two black criminals whom retired detective Joshua Burke (James Earl Jones) blackmails into job-training an inner-city group of black youngsters. By the end of the film, Durrell and Anderson have acquired a sense of responsibility toward the students and the community.

Poitier obviously sought audience appeal by including well-known and popular black performers like Jones, Denise Nicholas, and Frances Foster. In this case, however, he did not use cameo appearances by popular black comedians to create hybrid minstrel caricatures. Instead, he used these well-known performers in serious roles that focused attention on the plight of the inner-city teenagers trying to acquire job skills and on Durrell's and Anderson's growing sense of social responsibility. The film thus dramatizes the social ideals, easily shared by ambitious whites, of black self-help and self-esteem. The well-dressed, obviously affluent, and masculine Durrell and Anderson become black role models as well as teachers for the group of unemployed black teenagers. In addition, the developing relationship between the two men and the teenagers represents the positive impact that two black thieves may have on the constructive development of black juveniles insofar as the thieves prepare black teenagers for the realities of seeking respectable jobs. Thus, *A Piece of the Action* performs the traditional function of African-American humor—to instruct the formerly objectified in-group rather than merely entertain the out-group or third party of a tendentious joke.[34] The film's narrative function, then, reflects the technique of unification since *A Piece of the Action* can be described as "ready repartees" against the socially irresponsible narratives of hybrid minstrel films.

Which Way Is Up? was the next important black-directed comedy to deviate from the hybrid minstrel form. *Which Way Is Up?* starred Richard Pryor in three roles. Michael Schultz directed and African-American novelist Cecil Brown wrote the first draft of the scenario, although the final draft was written by Carl Gottlieb, a white scenarist, and produced by Steve Krantz, a white.

From A Piece of the Action. *Courtesy of the Museum of Modern Art Film Stills Archive.*

Even though *Which Way Is Up?* uses some elements of hybrid minstrelsy, it examines serious social issues. The film focuses on Leroy Jones (Pryor), who initially works as an orange picker but graduates to the position of company foreman. Jones is torn between supporting his fellow workers' attempts to better their working conditions at the possible cost of his job and his own need to maintain two homes—one for his wife and one for his mistress and their child. In addition, Jones is fearful that Mr. Mann, the president of Agrico Industries, will murder him if he does not keep the workers' productivity at a high level. Even though both his wife, Annie Mae (Margaret Avery), and his lover, Vanetta (Vonetta McKee), leave him, Leroy decides that he no longer wants a job that forces him into the exploitative position of an overseer of Chicano and African-American laborers.

Several elements of this film are borrowed from the hybrid minstrel caricatures seen in such films as *Cotton Comes to Harlem.* For example, Richard Pryor performs three different hybrid minstrel roles—Leroy Jones, a cowardly young man; Reverend Thomas, a philandering minister; and Rufus Jones, Leroy's quarrelsome father. These comic roles clearly incorporate some traditional qualities of stage and screen coons. Such resemblances expand the film's audience, some of whom will assimilate these images and view the film as a hybrid minstrel form.

From Which Way Is Up? *Courtesy of the Museum of Modern Art Film Stills Archive.*

The film, however, also describes a serious social issue in which Jones as a fruit picker and later as foreman is caught between the union movement and the company's anti-union sentiment. Since he wishes to survive economically, Leroy at first demonstrates "coon" qualities by his obsequious behavior. Here, the performance represents simultaneity, appropriation, and transmission of the coon stereotype without assimilation. That is, Jones does not believe what he acts out. As the film continues, Jones grows into a black action hero who verbally assaults his white employer. He tells the president of Agrico Industries, "Been watching me, Mr. Mann?" Mann replies, "I dropped by to see how you were handling yourself, Leroy. Actually, you've done your usual incompetent job." In an instance of self-assertion, Leroy says, "You hired the wrong nigger for this job, and you gonna have to explain that to somebody, 'cause I just quit. Get my drift, boy? Now, here's the keys to your house and your doggone car. . . . I'm at the bottom of my life, Mr. Mann, and the only way for me is up. And if you don't like that, you better shoot me in my back right now 'cause that's the last part you ever gonna see of me. Big shot."[35]

The film's narrative closure critically assesses Leroy's emasculation by his white boss Mr. Mann—"the Man"—who gives Leroy nothing more than material rewards, a false sense of pride in his foreman's position, and enough money to support two households. When Leroy loses his friends, his wife, and his lover, he returns the material objects and position that falsely define his middle-class status—a house, a car, and his managerial position. Leroy's twist of fate makes this film an unusual example of an African-American comedy film that manipulates hybrid minstrel elements while it examines serious social issues.

The marketing strategy of *Which Way Is Up?* reveals the caution the industry employs when it distributes African-American comedy films that emphasize social problems. At first, producer Steve Krantz tried to ensure a favorable outcome by employing a successful black director. Michael Schultz agreed to direct an American remake of *The Seduction of Mimi*, an Italian film that was commercially successful when released five years earlier in Italy and America. Then Krantz sought to guarantee popularity by hiring Pryor to play the lead. Not only was Pryor a box-office star but, at the time, he had a four-film contract with Universal Studios. When Pryor requested that Cecil Brown be hired to rewrite the scenario, Krantz agreed but later replaced Brown with Carl Gottlieb, a veteran scenarist at Universal.[36] Pryor probably agreed to have the final script prepared by an established scenarist. Krantz thus collected the necessary talent for the film's production "package," which Universal Studios agreed to finance and distribute.

The way a studio chooses to market a film usually determines its box-office success. Fearing that *Which Way Is Up?* would not appeal to the white audience, Universal Studios relegated the film to second-string theaters in African-American neighborhoods in some cities where the film played.[37] Nevertheless, *Which Way Is Up?* "grossed more than any other black [commercial] film, a whopping $19 million" with a production cost of $3.2 million.[38] Since some of these second-string theaters were located in downtown urban areas like Forty-Second Street in New York and State Street in Chicago, whites might have been attracted to the film.

Since *Which Way Is Up?* was an interracial collaboration, race cannot be assumed to determine the production of a racially non-tendentious African-American comedy film. However, according to a Bakhtin analysis of discourse and in accordance with the function of race in hybrid minstrel comedy, the determination lies in the choice of the dominant tendentious form or the internally persuasive discourse of the objectified black. In this sense, I argue that race is a function of ideology, not a function of the producer, director, or writer. I will elaborate on the ideological function of race below.

A Piece of the Action and *Which Way Is Up?* prove that, during a period of declining production of black commercial films, certain talented African-Americans were able to direct and write a few black comedies that employed the technique of unification to address serious social issues. Significantly, a black comedy that incorporated both hybrid minstrelsy elements and serious social issues grossed more than most other black-oriented films. At the same time, the black comedies that included serious social issues and no minstrelsy did not gross as well as the "purer"—that is, less ideologically and critically explicit—hybrid minstrel black comedies. The narrative structure of hybrid minstrel films works within a racially dualistic system. In its satiric subtype, seen in the film *Which Way Is Up?,* hybrid minstrel narrative strategies decode and reverse the narrative structure of the initial racist poetics of blackface minstrel comedy.

Robert Townsend's *Hollywood Shuffle* exemplifies the process of reversal that employs the technique of unification. "The joke depends—whether entirely or in part—on the fact that a clerk [actor Robert Townsend] is making use of analogies taken from the domain of his everyday activities. But the bringing of these abstractions [sketches] into connection with the ordinary things with which his life is normally filled [Hollywood's use of racial stereotypes] is an act of unification."[39] The narrative structure of *Hollywood Shuffle* is a collection of stereotyped experiences that black performers encounter in Hollywood. The purpose of the narrative is to ridicule both whites and blacks who produce, perform, and direct racially tendentious films. This is quite evident in the sketch that dramatizes a casting call for Eddie Murphy character types. The use of the unification technique is equally apparent in Keenen Ivory Wayan's *I'm Gonna Git You Sucka!* (UA, 1988), whose narrative evokes laughter by parodying black action films of the 1970s.

We must also consider cultural and ideological forces that are not so obvious and whose connotative elements construct gender, sexuality, class, and race. The text functions as the occasion as much as the site for these constructions, since they require the "active," rather than "inactive" participation of a listener-viewer and the objectified group. This audience, responding to their own individual socioeconomic and sociopsychic desires, adopts spectatorial positions and consumes filmed and televised minstrels. African-American comedy exhibits several forms and the reception of this comedy also has several modes. Although this is not an exhaustive list, an audience may assimilate and accept the authorized narrative, it may appropriate the fundamental sentiments through mediation, or it may perform an oppositional reading that denies authorized and mediated discourses.

Minstrel comedy film has undergone a series of transformations but none that have neutralized its tendentious nature. The transition from blackface minstrelsy to hybrid minstrelsy and then to the satiric hybrid form has not changed its inherently racist and tendentious quality, which reflects its minstrel sources. A racially non-tendentious form of African-American comedy film would be rooted in a type of black folk humor that has undergone a similar sociopsychological transformation as blackface minstrelsy. The spectatorial relationships for black folk humor are as numerous as they are for minstrel forms. Critical analysis of this black folk humor must also be vigilant to detect any essentialist valorization of race that permits criticism to objectify other forms of black subjectivity such as gender, sexuality, and class.

This discussion of race as a function of ideology, and of African-American comedy film as a distinct genre, has included analysis of the industrial, narrative, and spectatorial aspects of African-American film comedy. The critique is sociopsychologically engendered and racial, but it resists the easy embrace of an *essentially* or *innately* African-American aesthetic that has somehow been suppressed by whites. African-Americans, like other oppressed groups, employ survival strategies for sociopsychic sustenance. My recognition of black survival strategies, however, does not assume a monolithic or monologic form of black resistance. There exists no singular African-American personality; African-Americans belong to a diverse community whose rich complexion equals its international breadth. Like the trickster, the community has polyphonic stratagems of resistance.

The popularity of African-American comedy films reflects the number of reading strategies an audience can use. Each of the three comic subtypes (hybrid minstrelsy, satiric hybrid minstrelsy, and urban black folk comedy) does not entirely cancel the elements of the others, which enables each subtype to attract a racially diverse audience. Spectators may not recognize the intertextuality of the three subtypes, but the shared comic elements of each subtype sustain a network of images. The familiar imagery evokes laughter from the audience and sustains the popularity of a certain narrative form. The relationship between African-American comedy film and its audience may be expressed as "the economy of expenditure" of the available receptions of a specific comedy subtype. There exists three forms: the dominant, the negotiated, and the oppositional; all of these reading positions are applicable to any of the three comedy subtypes.

Toward a Critical Theory of African-American Film

The theory that I am proposing assumes an interracial audience. This theory resists privileging narratives, such as the satiric hybrid minstrel form, which reverse racial hierarchies. The theory also resists valorizing racial dualism within the conventional comedy, family, and action film genres and their respective subtypes. In the following chapter, I will use this theory to demystify the naturalizing effects of racism as well as to analyze the sexist and homophobic elements of African-American film. According to this theory, polyphonic spectatorial relationships avoid racial dualisms that may be present in black-oriented films. Correspondingly, this theory resists the notion that certain processes of production (such as independent filmmaking or the studio distribution of films) determine how a black-oriented film is received by an audience. Thus, my theory argues for the polyphonic nature of reception, which permits dialogue within any genre, between genres, and among the viewers of African-American film.[40]

Systemically speaking, the "other" remains racially inflected as long as the dominant narrative form, blackface minstrelsy, exists within the imagination of the producer and the spectator-listener. Consequently, the theoretical importance of a theory of reception is central to an analysis of the production of minstrelsy, its hybrid forms, and urban black folk comedy.

The theory of African-American comedy described in this essay combines Sigmund Freud's notion of unification, Jurij Lotman's indeterminate quality of the language code, and Michel Foucault's understanding of the social nature of the dominant. The Freudian notion of unification permits rebellion in the satiric hybrid minstrelsy, but this rebellion is premised on the existence of a "natural" white patriarchal order that the radicals want to reverse. I consider any "natural" order as a mythic construction that has been affected by sociopsychical and socioeconomic processes.[41] Again, I propose a nonstatic theory of African-American film which is modeled on a perpetual struggle rather than a social contract "regulating a transaction or the conquest of a territory." The power

held by the film industry and inherent in the receptive process is practiced "rather than possessed; it is not the 'privilege' of the dominant
class, but the overall effect of its strategic positions."[42] Accordingly,
authoritarian discourses are dependent on a network of relations that
are neither natural, heavenly, or static. African-American film comedy
subtypes in particular, and their facsimiles in other genres, result from a
social consensus that is neither "natural," god-given, or eternal.

Any narrative structure of African-American film, and its reception
by any spectator, requires a two-fold process of analysis. African-
American comedy film comprises blackface, hybrid, and satiric minstrel
forms, as well as urban black folk comedy, which is a racially non-
tendentious humor. Minstrel forms are structurally similar to a racially
tendentious joke. Ideologically, the satiric subtype has reformist properties (like the technique of unification) because these comedies fail to
question the use of racially demeaning images. All three minstrel types
validate an authoritative form—racial essentialist narratives against
which minstrel forms are impotent in their rebellions. For example, both
Which Way Is Up? and *Hollywood Shuffle* use coonlike elements that
evoke minstrel humor. The overall rebellious character of *Hollywood
Shuffle* has not changed from its "Amos 'n' Andy" beginnings. Such
protests reflect "an effect that is manifested and sometimes extended by
the position of those who are dominated."[43] But this cannot be viewed as
an unmediated discourse accepted by an audience. Psychoanalysis alone
provides an inadequate interpretation of the sociopsychic and socioeconomic elements that structure American race relations and determine
how race is dramatized in African-American film.

3

Family Film

Black Writers in Hollywood

This chapter describes how interracial collaboration in the film industry permitted black writers to appropriate the family film narrative and infuse it with black-oriented sociopolitical content. *Take a Giant Step* (UA, 1959) and *A Raisin in the Sun* (Columbia, 1961) implicitly contested blackface minstrel family films, such as *Hallelujah* (1929), which avoid dramatizing issues of race, gender, and class. Second, the chapter describes how black artists use techniques to permit audience identification with black characters and how the relationship between the black spectator and black filmic imagery permits the assimilation of a unified black hero in works such as *The Learning Tree* (Warner, 1969). Black writers also selectively subvert the conventional values of the family melodrama. The production history of the *A Raisin in the Sun* (Columbia, 1959) screenplay illustrates how a black writer appropriates a master form for subversive ends. Black writers also have used narrative form and camera techniques to undermine conventional discourse and classical film narratives. In chapter seven, I discuss how *Bush Mama* (Haile Gerima, 1975) resists the integrationist mode of black family film and disrupts the fluidity of its narrative to deny middle-class identification. This chapter on the family film, however, focuses on Hollywood's image of the black family and the industry's provisions for black participation.

Blackface minstrelsy, hybrid minstrelsy, and satiric hybrid minstrelsy are the key elements of three subtypes of African-American family film—blackface, hybrid, and satiric hybrid family films. Each subtype invites different forms of black subjectivity and different relationships between the audience and the screen image. A critical study of black family film which analyzes the film studio, the black artist, the film, and its reception reveals the problems facing studios who market black films. It also explains why film studios limit black films to low production budgets.

Blackface minstrel family films (hereafter referred to as blackface family film) include individual family members who exhibit composite racial stereotypes. In such films as *Hallelujah, The Green Pastures* (1936), and *Cabin in the Sky* (1943) family members exhibit modernized versions of nineteenth-century racial stereotypes—the obese matriarch or mammy figure, her inarticulate henpecked mate or sambo, sex-crazed black bucks, exotic primitives, and tragic mulattoes caught in an interracial maelstrom.[1] Post–World War II black family films presented softened versions of these stereotypes.

The hybrid minstrel family film, a second subtype, is any variation on the traditional minstrel stereotype. The 1949 film *Pinky* is one illustration of this hybrid form. *Pinky* features Ethel Waters as both a loyal black maidservant and the grandmother (or grand mammy) of Pinky, a mulatto played by Jeanne Crain. Pinky exhibits certain features of the tragic mulatto stereotype, since she is caught between celebrating and denying her racial heritage and is rejected by both racial communities. The narrative humanizes the mulatto stereotype, however, through a racially uplifting closure—Pinky rejects a life of racial passing and commits herself to the betterment of the black race. Because the film valorizes a racially dualistic world, Pinky cannot celebrate her mixed racial background. She must affirm her African-American heritage and, thereby, deny her Euro-American parent. Interestingly, she returns to her "grand mammy" and establishes a black nursing school. Pinky, as an agent of racial dualism, cannot contest the racially segregated education practices that forced her to enroll in a northern nursing school.

Since *Pinky* retains many offensive characterizations—Waters as the loyal mammy, Nina Mae McKinney as a razor-toting primitive, and Frederick O'Neal as Nina's lazy, conniving lover—and since *Pinky* is a vehicle of separate-but-equal educational policies, this film resembles *Hallelujah.* Although *Pinky* does not describe a world devoid of racism as does *Hallelujah,* its filmic construction of black life is as shortsighted as her educational reform. The film overlooks the problem of an almost-white heroine who becomes the savior of an educationally disfranchised black community. Pinky's mixed racial parentage parallels the film narrative's mixed ideological function, since the narrative assimilates racial stereotypes previously circulated by the genre. *Pinky* caters to audiences who accept black stereotypes but who, in their newfound liberalism, accept a modified version of the tragic mulatto when performed by a white actress such as Jeanne Crain.

From Pinky. *Courtesy of the Museum of Modern Art Film Stills Archive.*

The third subtype, the satiric hybrid black family film, is produced by major studios and written by African-Americans who adapt their literary works for film. The satiric hybrid film uses the formal structure of traditional family melodrama to frame its politicized portrayals of black life and experiences. The use of the term satiric hybrid sums up the ironic and neo-colonial nature of the relationship between black writers, the black text, and film studio executives. The satiric hybrid and neocolonial subtypes rhetorically question the validity and function of blackface and hybrid black-oriented family melodramas like *Hallelujah* and *Pinky*. In short, the two subtypes satirize and parody the melodramatic tradition that locates black family narratives within a middle-class entertainment mode.

The African-American family film genre existed more than a decade before the 1929 appearance of King Vidor's *Hallelujah!,* a southern black-oriented family film. In fact, African-Americans produced, wrote, and directed some of the earliest black family films. The writers of these family films also performed other duties. For example, Rev. W. S. Smith, a black Baptist preacher, wrote the scenario for the Frederick Douglass Film Company production *The Colored American, or Winning His Suit* (1916). *The Colored American* resembled Lincoln family films (discussed in chapter one) insofar as the film dealt with a black hero who proves his worth and ultimately returns to his black family. The Lincoln Motion Picture Company's *The Realization of a Negro's Ambition* (1916) and *The Trooper of Company K* (1916) were written by Noble M. Johnson, the studio's president and male lead. This motion picture firm was probably one of the first African-American film outfits to have its president and featured actor write its scenarios. Lincoln's division of labor resembles the organizational framework of a film collective in which members perform more than one task.

Adaptations from black literary classics provided another source for the construction of the African-American family film. When film companies adapted popular, black literary works for the screen, they were confident of attracting a literate black audience. In May 1917, the Frederick Douglass Company premiered a Paul Laurence Dunbar film adaptation of his short story *The Scapegoat*. The production of *The Scapegoat* pioneered screen adaptations of African-American literary works and was followed by Micheaux's screen adaptation of his first novel, *The Homesteader.* Micheaux also adapted Charles Chesnutt's 1900 novel *The House Behind the Cedars* (1923). The combination of a black literary classic and the theme of African-American family life became the menu for black prestige pictures such as *Native Son* (1951, 1986), *A Raisin In the Sun, The Learning Tree, The River Niger* (1976), *The Color Purple* (1985), and the teleplay *The Women of Brewster Place* (1989). All of the above literary works were written by blacks but widely read by both black and white Americans. Thus, even the early black independent producers preferred to make screen adaptations from black literary classics with proven crossover appeal.

The early black independent film producers not only established an African-American family film genre, they also employed blacks to write scenarios. This practice allowed black film productions to express a black perspective in both their aural and visual languages as well as their production strategies. I refer to this strategy (the employment of black technicians and writers to create black-oriented films) as a "black mode of production." This mode of production increases the degree of black participation in the construction of the film. The term has little to do with the film's "political" vision or its reflection of a "black aesthetic."

Literary Forces Encouraging the Use of Black Writers

Hollywood did not produce black family films written by African-American writers until the late 1950s. The new opportunities for black film writers in Hollywood resulted in part from studio interest in film adaptations and partly from Hollywood's recognition of the popularity of African-American literature. The industry's preference for screen adaptations of popular works is evidenced by the Academy of Motion Picture Arts and Sciences 1956 creation of the Best Writing Award for the Best Adapted Screenplay. This move affected the subject matter and themes that studio films would choose to dramatize.[2]

Between 1940 and 1960 one short story and a few novels by African-Americans had received such acclaim that film studios decided to adapt them for the screen. Frank Yerby's best seller, *The Foxes of Harrow* (1946), was produced by Twentieth Century–Fox in 1947. Willard Motley's two novels *Knock on Any Door* (1947) and *Let No Man Write My Epitaph* (1958) were produced by Columbia in 1949 and 1960, respectively. MGM produced *Bright Road* (1953), a screen adaptation of Mary E. Vroman's short story "See How They Run" (1951).

Moreover, black-oriented dramas written by African-Americans were increasingly accepted by mainstream American theaters and professional critics during the 1950s. In 1953, Louis Peterson's *Take a Giant Step* appeared on Broadway. *Take a Giant Step* was revived off-Broadway in 1956 and received critical acclaim. The off-Broadway Greenwich Mews Theatre produced William Branch's historical dramatization of John Brown and Frederick Douglass, *In Splendid Error* (1954). Alice Childress's satire on black stereotypes, *Trouble in Mind* (1957), and Loften Mitchell's dramatic treatment of school desegregation in *A Land Beyond the River* (1957) were also produced for the stage. In 1959, the most significant event of the decade for black theater occurred when Hansberry received the Critics Circle Award for *A Raisin in the Sun.*[3]

By the end of the fifties, major studios were hiring African-Americans to write scenarios for studio-produced black-oriented films. With the integration of black writers came more pressure for studios to broaden their depiction of African-American life and experiences. The development of a third subtype of African-American family film is the result of the hiring of black scenarists, the increasing popularity of black-oriented film fare, and the impact of the civil rights movement.

The literary exchange between studio executives and black writers during this period resembles the relationship that newly independent African nations enjoyed with their former colonial administrators. The black writer, like the newly independent African nation, was still beholden to the system of production, distribution, and consumption. Individual writers or nations could not disrupt the flow and if they tried, other blacks would eagerly replace them. In fact, the film industry now engaged in a sort of neocolonial relationship between black artists, their audience, and mass-produced black art. Only through the processes of negotiation and resistance could African-American writers and white studio executives generate a filmic portrait of the African-American family. On the one hand, this neocolonial relationship usually ensured that formal conventions were respected. On the other hand, black scenarists used subversive rhetorical strategies that obscured the over-determined nature of the American film industry, which demanded adherence to the generic form. For example, in accordance with the requirements of the film industry, most early black-authored family films, such as *Take a Giant Step, The Learning Tree,* and *Black Girl* (1972), focus on the qualities of one family member.

During this period, there were a few short-lived rebels who penned scenarios that broke with the genre's insistent focus on one member of the family. *A Raisin in the Sun* and *The River Niger* brought attention to the dreams of individual family members and thereby revealed the genre's ability to speak to a multitude of black others whose voices were not confined to one black hero(ine). The neocolonial partnership between studio and black writer requires one to study how the industry packages a black-authored film for consumption by an audience. This requirement is as important as a close reading of the film text. Film analysis must include descriptions of the industry, the product, and consumer-related issues as well as aesthetic concerns that involve the relationship between film and spectator.

Regardless of the film industry's assumption of an "average" African-American moviegoer and attempts to market films to such, black audiences employ different reading strategies based on their class, ethnicity, gender, and sexual orientation. Even within the limited confines of neocolonial black film production, the reactions of black *or* white audiences are far from predetermined. Finally, the reception of this subtype is equally indeterminate if one views these films as examples of the disjointed nature of products issued from a relationship between the colonizer (the master or patriarchal discourse) and the colonized (those bound to masters or confined within a patriarchal system).

The interplay between conventional and "black" constructions of the American family is present in the popular construction of the African-American family. It is through the African-American family film that dominant discourses of race, nation, gender, and sexuality are dramatized and contested in front of and behind the camera as well as behind the desks of film executives. In analyzing the film industry's marketing of *Take a Giant Step* and *A Raisin in the Sun,* I describe the neocolonial relationship that two studios and two black artists encounter.[4] I argue that major studios determined the form and black scenarists employed writerly techniques to resist some of the formal requirements of the traditional family melodrama—requirements that erase racial differences or create racial stereotypes. The black-authored family film is thereby formally constructed around a male-headed household or the *desire for* a patriarchal presence. Yet, some of these films express several realities that conjoin differences of race, gender, and class.

Take a Giant Step

Louis Peterson's *Take a Giant Step* is an example of a black family film that was written by a black but was produced by a major studio. Forty years after Micheaux adapted his novel *The Homesteader* for a film, black dramatist Peterson (with white colleague Julius J. Epstein) adapted his 1953 Broadway play for the screen. Epstein, a former Warner Brothers contract writer, was a prestigious Hollywood writer who had received a 1942 Academy Award (with his brother Philip and Howard Koch) for writing the Best Screenplay (*Casablanca,* Warner).

Take a Giant Step was produced by the independent company Hecht-Hill-Lancaster. Organized in 1947 by Burt Lancaster and producer Harold Hecht, the company gained Hollywood's attention in 1955 with *Marty* (UA), Paddy Chayefsky's screen adaptation of his play, which had first appeared on a television program in 1953. The film won the Academy's Best Picture Award, Best Director Award (Delbert Mann), Best Actor Award (Ernest Borgnine), and Best Screenplay Award (Chayefsky). Undoubtedly encouraged by the reputation of Epstein, the producer, and the production company, United Artists agreed to release *Giant Step.*[5]

Thus, *Giant Step* was the cumulative result of several necessities of supply and demand. First, there was the increasing popularity and mainstream critical acceptance of black literary works. Second, there existed a low supply of film products and the high demand for novel "first-grade films." Third, independent producers wished to supply this need for novel films that addressed contemporary issues. Fourth, Hollywood distributors such as United Artists agreed to work and distribute the films of independent producers such as Hecht-Hill-Lancaster.[6] Finally, many of the first-run, downtown theaters had been increasingly losing their white audiences and attracting more black moviegoers.[7] Regardless of these changes, *Take a Giant Step* and its producer Epstein experienced many of the formidable problems that black-oriented films would encounter in the succeeding years.

In *Take a Giant Step,* Johnny Nash, a popular rock-and-roll singer, portrays Spencer Scott, a black teenager growing up in a northern white community. The film addresses problems Spencer encounters in white society and with his father Lem Scott, who refuses to empathize with Spencer's frustrations. (Frederick O'Neal, a cofounder of the American Negro Theatre, played the father in the film as he had done on Broadway.)

Spencer's main racial problem is his white teacher's interpretation of black slaves as being "too lazy" to fight for their emancipation. Spencer refutes his teacher's interpretation and is expelled from school. His father upholds the authority of the teacher, and Spencer is left without a parental figure to support him. It would seem that the film passively complied with the familiar aspects of the adolescent-parental conflict subgenre of the family film. Spencer's heroism was at least one Afro-centric element that the film does not avoid despite the father's attitude toward the ignorant white teacher.[8] Spencer is portrayed neither as a coon nor a Tom, yet he must subordinate himself. His accommodation occurs after he defies a white figure of authority. Spencer does not merely represent an individual black adolescent, he represents the experiences of the African-American community.

Whether the American film industry was ready to approve of Spencer's profanity became a major problem that momentarily stalled the film's distribution. A *Variety* article, entitled "True-to-Life Cussing May Deny Seal for *Take a Giant Step*," reported that the film "may be released sans an MPAA Production Code seal, according to producer Harold Hecht, who prexies [is the president of the] company." The article went on to report that if the Motion Picture Association of America did not give *Giant Step* a Production Code seal, Hecht-Hill-Lancaster would limit the film's release to "adult showings in first-run situations and not worry about the seal."

Hecht stated that the "subject matter is so frankly handled—and with dialog carrying such words as 'hell,' 'bastard,' and 'prostitute,'—that it's extremely doubtful that official sanction will be forthcoming."[9] On March 18, 1959, United Artists had not agreed to distribute the production. United Artists's non-exclusive releasing pact with Hecht's company suggested, however, that there *was* a possibility that UA would release *Giant Step*. Hecht assumed that United Artists would release the film and believed that the Broadway opening of *A Raisin in the Sun* (March 11, 1959) would "spark interest in *Giant Step*." Hecht's belief may have reflected his hope to recoup the film's estimated $300,000 production cost; but this suggests only one effect that *Raisin* had on Hecht's hopes for *Giant Step*.

Race, Sexuality, and a Black Matinee Idol

Contrary to Hecht's hopes, *Raisin*'s Broadway success had little effect on UA's promotion and distribution of *Giant Step*. Co-scenarist Epstein, in a 1960 *Variety* article, accused UA of insufficiently promoting the film. Epstein believed UA shelved *Giant Step* even though the film had been well received by *Saturday Review of Literature* and *Newsweek* critics.[10] Epstein added, "United Artists is having no part of racial problem pictures . . . and *Take A Giant Step* is simply going to keep gathering dust and anonymity." In the same *Variety* article, Harry Hendel, president of Western Pennsylvania Allied Theatres Association, interpreted UA's inactivity differently. According to *Variety,* Hendel

> protested strongly as to [Epstein's] . . . remarks, declaring them unfair to United Artists. He said the picture had bookings around the country to do business. He mentioned Detroit as one of the bigger cities where it did very little at the box office.
>
> He also said that the picture had some bookings in this area [Pittsburgh and Philadelphia] but people just weren't buying unknown Negro performers as serious actors. He mentioned Harry Belafonte and Sidney Poitier as being the only Negroes strong enough to carry a picture at the b.o.

The absence of a youth-oriented black star may have been the result of the American film industry's promotion of the white rebellious youth. Although many white actors and actresses including Marlon Brando, James Dean, Sal Mineo, Natalie Wood, and Anne Francis appeared in fifties pictures such as *The Wild One* (Columbia, 1953), *Blackboard Jungle* (MGM, 1955), and *Rebel without a Cause* (Warner Brothers, 1955) and portrayed a variety of male and female types, African-Americans were apparently limited to Sidney Poitier. Poitier was the adult-oriented star in *No Way Out* (Fox, 1950) who, five years later, played a juvenile delinquent in *The Blackboard Jungle*. The elasticity of Poitier's role and age expresses the paucity of roles for black male leads in American films. His roles were respectable and as sexually antiseptic as a eunuch. Poitier's roles measure the limits of black masculinity. This analysis is strengthened by a critique of Hollywood's treatment of Poitier's ever-sensual contemporary—Harry Belafonte.

During the same period, Belafonte's sensuality both titillated and frightened his audiences. The industry, regardless of *Island in the Sun*'s (Fox, 1957) $8 million gross at a production cost of $2,250,000, did not want a black Marlon Brando in 1957.[11] Robert H. Welker noted:

> with "Island in the Sun" . . . another giant step was taken—two interracial love affairs, frankly avowed, and including that ultimate trauma to many a white male psyche, a white woman in love with a colored man, and not merely ready but eager for his touch. Again, there were compromises: the unidentified British setting, the absence of full-blooded interracial kisses, the breakup of the colored man's affair through fear of prejudice.[12]

Welker's observation underlines the important limitations that adult-oriented film imposed on the black hero and white heroine in their

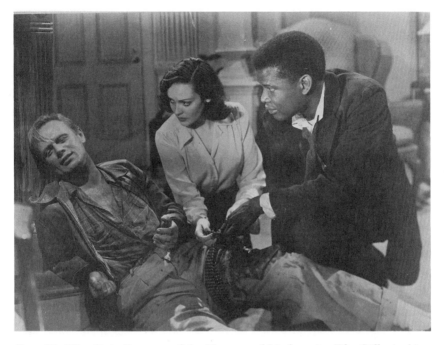

From No Way Out. *Courtesy of the Museum of Modern Art Film Stills Archive.*

dramatization of interracial intimacy. Recalling the fact that Micheaux had pioneered this effort in the early twenties, the change in the dramatization of interracial intimacy in major studio-produced films is apparent.

Hollywood also restricted the emergence of the youth and adult-oriented black protagonist because the American film industry had not yet developed major black stars. During the fifties and early sixties, the black hero was limited to the contours of one actor—Sidney Poitier.

If Belafonte could not visually portray his sexuality in the adult-oriented film *Island in the Sun,* it follows that Nash's portrayal of adolescent sexuality in the teen picture *Giant Step* would not be accepted, even if his love were directed toward a black woman. The mass audience could not accept black sexuality unless it was portrayed in a violent or primitive manner, for example, the dramatization of alleged interracial rape in *Sergeant Rutledge* (Warner, 1960) and *To Kill a Mockingbird* (Universal, 1962), or the depiction of sexual hedonism within a black community in *Carmen Jones* (Twentieth Century–Fox, 1954) and *Porgy and Bess* (Columbia, 1959). Black sexuality that was limited to the "primitive" black community or to alleged rapes by black men could be psychically sanctioned by whites if the assaults resulted in a threatened racial lynching of an innocent black man.

From Island in the Sun. *Courtesy of the Museum of Modern Art Film Stills Archive.*

At this cultural moment, there did not exist any humane portrayal of black sexuality by Hollywood. There were other factors, too, which inhibited the cinematic portrayal of African-American life. Film exhibitors felt that black-oriented films should be booked chiefly in black populated areas. Theater managers elsewhere feared that booking black-oriented films would attract blacks and scare away the theater's regular white audience.

Nevertheless, the major problem that *Giant Step* faced was the heroic ambition of Spencer Scott, who defied the ignorance of a northern white teacher and explored his awakening sexual desires. Although *Giant Step* may not have been an interesting film for a mass audience, it did give African-American youths an image of a defiant black kid who refused his ignorant white teacher's attempt to dehumanize the African-American community. In this sense, *Giant Step* is a great leap toward liberating black heroism from Hollywood's social and economic restrictions.

Giant Step preceded *A Raisin in the Sun* by six years in its Broadway production and by two years as a Hollywood independent feature film. The two plays dramatized the growing black consciousness among the younger generation of educated, northern-born, black teenagers. The

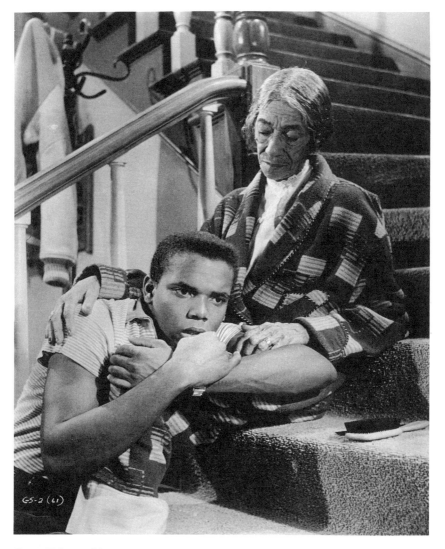

From Take a Giant Step. *Courtesy of the Museum of Modern Art Film Stills Archive.*

films also portrayed residential integration by middle-class black families. There exist in both films the memories of a southern past held, for
example, by the maid Christine in *Giant Step* and Lena Younger in
Raisin. In their formal structure and depiction of a three-generation
black urban family, the two plays and their film adaptations continued

From Take a Giant Step. *Courtesy of the Museum of Modern Art Film Stills Archive.*

the modernist black-family melodrama developed by Theodore Ward in *The Big White Fog* (1938). Ward's play represented black life during the Depression era and raised the issues of poverty, unemployment, racial discrimination, and intraracial rivalry between Marcus Garveyites and Communists and between black entrepreneurs and black laborers.

The three plays, *The Big White Fog, Take a Giant Step,* and *A Raisin in the Sun,* and the two films *Giant Step* and *Raisin* exemplify a black literary movement in which pioneer writers struggled to develop their craft and portray the social psychology of the African-American middle-class family. In the mid-sixties, the Black Arts movement competed with the modernist-integrationist textual tradition of Wards, Peterson, and Hansberry and established a black nationalist protest style epitomized by the dramas of LeRoi Jones's (Amiri Baraka) *Dutchman* (1967), Joseph A. Walker's *The River Niger,* and the independent black films of the late seventies.[13] Thus, the film adaptation of *Raisin* is a profound reflection of African-American modernist drama. Its place in film history is further assured in that it is the first screenplay written solely by a black woman.

A Raisin in the Sun

One of the earliest major examples of a black family film that was written by a black scenarist and independently produced for a major studio is the David Susskind and Philip Rose Production of *A Raisin in the Sun*. The film was directed by Daniel Petrie, and Hansberry adapted her original play for the screen.

Susskind was interested in producing *Raisin* because he recognized that it would be a financially and critically successful Broadway play. *Variety*'s coverage of the play's pre-Broadway tryouts was one way in which Susskind may have developed an interest in *Raisin*. On 28 January 1959, *Variety* reported,

> Whatever the theatre shortage in Gotham may be, there must be room for "A Raisin in the Sun." Already of solid substance in tryout form, the Lorraine Hansberry drama is loaded with smash potentials that should ripen into substantial Broadway tenancy.

Variety also heralded the fact that the play was "written, directed and acted by Negroes, (with only one white role in the cast)." This mode of production, which entailed black control over three major aspects of dramatic art, was adopted by a mainstream American entertainment institution—Broadway. Later, Hollywood would institute a similar mode of production and thereby rejuvenate the black commercial film movement within the dominant structure of Hollywood studios.

The content of *Raisin* seemed to be far different from the content of plays made by whites about blacks, and *Variety* hinted at this: " 'Raisin' stands out as a shining example of talent potential if given the opportunity. The play should draw comment not only for the quality of its presentation but also for the depth of its message."

On March 11, 1959, *Raisin* opened on Broadway and received rave reviews. Two days later, Susskind wrote to Sam Briskin, Columbia Pictures vice-president in charge of production, and expressed his interest in a screen adaptation of *Raisin*. Susskind wrote:

> I have an inside track on this property as a consequence of my relationship with the author and her attorney. I think if you were to manifest real interest I could be granted a pre-empt right on the play for motion pictures at the best price offered by any competitor. At this writing, United Artists, Harry Belafonte, Metro-Goldwyn-Mayer, Paramount, Fox, Hall-Bartlett and the Mirisch Brothers have expressed strong interest in purchasing the play.[14]

At this early date, at least six major film producers were interested in a screen adaptation of the play. Susskind, writing in the same letter, recognized that the play presented "a warm, frequently amusing and profoundly moving story of [N]egro life in which, *for once,* the race issue is not paramount." He reassured Briskin that a film version featuring Poitier would attract an audience: "after *The Defiant Ones* and the upcoming *Porgy and Bess,* Sidney Poitier would be an important box office element."

By the 16th of March, Briskin wrote "we [Columbia] have had this interest . . . since we first learned of the play and its pre-New York openings . . . we have been approached by others both in and out of the studio."[15] Before a month had passed, *Variety* reported on 1 April 1959 that Columbia Pictures in association with Susskind and Rose had acquired the film rights to *Raisin* for $300,000. Susskind formulated the preproduction package that had been accepted by the studio. The package included himself and Rose as co-producers, Hansberry as scenarist, Poitier as featured star, and costars Claudia McNeil, Ruby Dee, and Diana Sands.

Martin Baum, the agent for Poitier and *Raisin*'s black stage-director Lloyd Richards, initially suggested that Richards direct the film version. Columbia's vice-president of publicity and advertising Paul Lazarus discussed this possibility with Briskin, who inquired about Richards's CBS-TV videotape production of *Raisin*. In a letter to Lazarus, Briskin reported that "when it got down to the last couple of days of rehearsal and the cameras were placed on the act he [Richards] seemed lost and CBS had to throw in a TV director to help him."[16]

Thus, Columbia refused to give Richards an opportunity to direct the film adaptation of the Broadway play that he directed. Columbia studio executives were both cautious and backward. They wanted to produce *Raisin* because of its financial and critical success, yet they did not want to make the same gamble that Broadway had made with Richards, one of the first blacks to direct a Broadway play. When Columbia executives approved Susskind's three-picture contract with director Daniel Petrie, *Raisin* had its director.[17] Petrie had made one film, *The Bramble Bush* (Warner, 1960), and was safe according to Columbia's standards.

Even though Columbia executives rejected Richards as the director, they accepted Hansberry as the scenarist. The primary reason that Columbia accepted Hansberry was *Raisin*'s status as a very hot property which gave its writer some leverage in deals with the studio. However, Briskin would not allow Hansberry any changes or additions to the screenplay which might threaten a mass audience. For example, Hansberry's first draft of the screenplay included Travis Younger having to bring fifty cents to school for special books about African-Americans. Columbia production executives Briskin and Arthur Kramer and the story editors William Fadiman and James Crow "agreed that this should be deleted from the screenplay," because it was not in the play. In addition, the Columbia production team "agreed that the addition of race issue material . . . should be avoided," because "the introduction of further race issues may lessen the sympathy of the audience, give the effect of propagandistic writing, and so weaken the story, not only as dramatic entertainment, but as propaganda too."[18]

The production team also sought to eliminate Beneatha's comment that "all Africans are revolutionaries today," calling it an example of "surplus in the race issue category and potentially troublesome to no purpose." In addition, executives argued that "Beneatha's dialogue about Africans needing salvation 'from the British and French' could give the picture needless trouble abroad."[19]

These suggested deletions are examples of the sort of censorship that occurs in Hollywood-produced and -distributed black commercial films. Since Hollywood films are produced for international markets and most black commercial films include social criticisms, studios usually tone down criticism of their potential audiences.

In *Raisin*'s case, Columbia story editors and executives were quick to reject Beneatha Younger's pan-African consciousness because their audience was not going to be limited to black pan-Africanists and white liberals like Susskind and Rose. Columbia's intended audience for *Raisin* included British and French colonialist sympathizers, and Columbia's recommended deletions acknowledged their presence. The audience for whom a black-oriented film is made determines film content and form and thus affects the filmic representation of black culture. Critics must identify the studio's estimation of an "intended audience" and describe and interpret the underlying ideology.

In the above instance, Columbia's executives suggested three deletions in *Raisin*'s sociopolitical and cultural elements. The power to delete certain ideological expressions of black culture highlights the limitations that Hollywood places on black scenarists and black directors involved in black commercial cinema. Film theoretician Gladstone Yearwood writes, "if the practice of black cinema is derived from that of Hollywood, then it will serve to reproduce the unequal relations characteristic of blacks in society."[20]

When black artists are involved in the mode of production as writers and directors, however, then these films become something other than mere Hollywood films. The presence of blacks in positions of power forces the critic to reformulate terms and elaborate new definitions. This critical process involves defining variables of image control (as in Beneatha's pan-African remarks, which were not cut) and determining the studio's actual exercised power. I use the term "colonized" to describe major studio productions, such as King Vidor's *Hallelujah* (MGM, 1929), which are written or solely directed by whites. In addition, I use the term "neocolonized" to refer to major studio productions, such as *Raisin,* which are written or directed by black people. These two categories distinguish the two forms of black-oriented major studio productions.

The critical success of the film adaptation of *Raisin* is demonstrated by the letters that Susskind received from people in the film and television industries. NBC special projects producer-director Robert K. Sharpe wrote,

> Perhaps more in this industry than any other we are judged by what we do when we have the opportunity to do it. In "Raisin in the Sun" I feel not only have you been loyal to a property which could have been changed in so many ways for expediency, but you and your associates have produced an even more immediate and compelling piece than the play itself. It is indeed a credit to the movie industry and certainly will be to this country overseas.[21]

This congratulatory letter conveys the prestige value *Raisin* had for its studio and the United States. However, the owner of William Goldman Theatres expressed an important reservation when he thanked Susskind: "We are presently in consultation with Columbia as to the best approach ad-wise in order to garner the greatest possible return at the box office. I am sure you realize that the picture does present a problem from a selling standpoint due to its subject matter. It is imperative that we reach a mass rather than just a class audience."[22] One way in which Columbia attempted to solve this problem, as well as exploit what Sharpe had discerned as "a credit to the movie industry," involved promoting *Raisin* as a prestige picture. Columbia made *Raisin* a United States entry in the 1961 Cannes Film Festival. The film thereby acquired an international prestige that grew when the festival gave *Raisin* a special award. The Screenwriters Guild also nominated it for the Best Screenplay of the Year award that same year. This award and nomination helped increase Hollywood's acceptance of black writers and the black family film genre.

On 10 January 1962, *Variety* reported that *Raisin*'s domestic rentals amounted to $1,100,000.[23] *Variety*'s estimated domestic rentals for *Raisin* nearly equaled Columbia Picture's $1,500,000 production costs reported in *Ebony* magazine.[24] Thus, *Raisin* was neither a financial disaster nor a box-office success. *Raisin* offered film studios proof that a low-budget, skillfully written black scenario about a black family which features well-known black performers can accrue prestige as well as return a moderate amount of money to its distributor. The film's effect on audiences and film critics, however, did not equal the play's critical acclaim and popularity among both black and white theater audiences. This imbalance may have resulted from the different expectations of theater and film audiences.

Major film productions like *Raisin* require mainstream audience approval, but theater productions like *Raisin* can attract an interracial audience and still focus on topics that would offend a mainstream film audience. It is understandable that the film had little effect on mainstream film audiences, and that most film critics ignored the importance of this film.

It is an unquestionable fact that the first priority of the film industry is to avoid products that threaten its major markets. Nonetheless, if one performs a close reading of the black family films adapted from African-American literary sources, one discovers the resiliency of the ongoing struggle that black writers have waged against dehumanized images of black family life.

Textual Dialogue in
A Raisin in the Sun

Like most committed black artists, Hansberry developed the story of the Younger family by experiencing its sociological equivalent. Hansberry attended Englewood High School on Chicago's southside, where she made friends with the black working-class youth who attended her school. James Baldwin wrote that "much of the strain under which Lorraine worked was produced by her knowledge of this reality, and her determined refusal not to be destroyed by it." Baldwin observed that he "had never in [his] life seen so many black people in the theatre. And the reason was that never before, in the entire history of the American theater, had so much of the truth of black people's lives been seen on [the Broadway] stage. Black people had ignored the theater because the theater had always ignored them."[25]

Granted, it is problematic to assert that an imaginative work like *Raisin* reflects the collective voices of working-class black America. But Hansberry's working film script generates a dialogic language that empowers a black working-class family in a particular region and at a particular time—post–World War II Chicago. The following discussion of the Youngers will serve as a case study of the filmic dramatization of political diversity within a black working-class family.

In *Raisin*, textual dialogism results from the family members who express different aspirations and political and religious beliefs. Lena's religious beliefs are an area of conflict between herself and her children. Walter Lee, her thirty-five-year-old son, wants to purchase a liquor store while Ruth, the wife of Walter Lee, considers abortion. Beneatha, Lena's daughter at college, freely questions the existence of God and the value of marriage.

Raisin attempts verbally and visually to affirm Afro-American working-class interests, especially through the two white male characters

From A Raisin in the Sun. *Courtesy of the Museum of Modern Art Film Stills Archive.*

who interact with Walter Lee and the Younger family. Mr. Arnold is the representative *sign* of white corporate America. His relationship to Walter is determined by the socioeconomic relationship between un-skilled, black America and a postindustrialized America. Walter repre-sents black men who live in northern, industrialized cities. Karl Lindner portrays the intra-class racial hostility of working-class American ethnics. Lindner's relationship to the Younger family signifies the white working-class that practices racially restrictive housing covenants that forbid blacks from purchasing homes in white neighborhoods. Thus, Lindner is the representative *sign* of this white collectivity. The inter-action between Lindner and the Youngers occasions a dialogic dis-course that wealthy Mr. Arnold and corporate America resist. *Raisin* explores linear mobility along class lines—the integration of predomi-nantly white working-class neighborhoods—but neglects or is unable to suggest an integration of the unskilled black into white corporate America.

The Younger family articulates desirous dream discourses that gener-ate an inter-familial dialogue. Lena's dreams encompass three different actions: placing $3000 in a savings account for her daughter's (Beneatha) medical school education, placing a $3500 down payment on a home for the Younger family, and giving her son $3500 to open a checking ac-count. It is Lena Younger's three-fold dream that includes the dreams of Beneatha, Ruth, and her deceased husband Big Walter. The promise of a medical school education for her college-trained daughter represents the advancement of black women. The purchase of a home for the Younger family shows a desire for better housing and permits the family melodrama to critically discuss the issue of racially segregated housing.

Raisin begins with Ruth Younger leaving the bedroom and entering the living room where her son, Travis, is asleep on the couch. Travis must sleep in the living room because there is not enough room in the two-bedroom apartment in which five family members live. Ruth awak-ens Travis and rushes him into the hallway bathroom that the Youngers share with their neighbors. Returning to the bedroom, she proceeds to do the same to her husband. He responds with two questions that reveal their marriage is "festering like a sore." Walter's first response questions the logic behind waking him up to go to a bathroom already occupied by his son. His second response illustrates his growing obsession with the $10,000 insurance money. He asks Ruth about the money and then asks her to persuade Lena to give him the insurance money so he can pur-chase a liquor store with his two friends Willie and Bobo. Ruth rejects Walter's request because she believes that the money belongs to Lena.

The opening dialogue and action establish that Walter Lee has dis-placed the collective Younger voice for that of an individual desire. Walter has assimilated the rhetoric of small business without its neces-sary requirement—experience and training. When Ruth rejects Walter's request, he counters with "I'm trying to talk to you about me!" Here, the reference "me" does not include the promise of a medical education for his sister Beneatha, nor does it include placing a down payment on a new home for the Younger family. Walter's desire does not encompass a group consciousness, and his entrepreneurial desire ignores the collective dreams that sustain the Younger family.

It is a bit obtuse to characterize Lena as a matriarch who dominates the members of her household. Throughout the play, Lena refers to her deceased husband Big Walter as an agent of her actions. Her son Walter Lee, on the other hand, repudiates Lena's dreams and the mythic qualities of Big Walter. In the assimilative mode, he constantly compares himself to wealthy Mr. Arnold and similar white men. Walter develops an entrepreneurial interest in a liquor store as a means to escape poverty and says that he must have the $10,000 insurance money that Lena will receive for the death of her husband.

The scene that presents Big Walter as the imaginary signifier of the black working-class and Lena as its poet takes place when Walter has left the apartment. Lena is "paying witness" to the memory of her deceased husband. She says, "You know Big Walter always hated the idea of being a servant. Always says man's hands wasn't meant to carry nobody's slop jars and make their beds. Always used to say they was meant to turn the earth with, make things. That husband of yours, Walter Lee, he's just like him." Lena's statement precedes a scene that presents Walter in his chauffeur uniform busily polishing Mr. Arnold's black limousine. The off-camera voice of Mr. Arnold is heard over a loud speaker: "Walter, bring the car around. Please." The camera follows Walter as he drives the car around the expanse of Mr. Arnold's mansion. Then the camera fades in on Walter rushing to open Mr. Arnold's car door. Arnold exits from the car, hands Walter a newspaper, leaves the camera frame, and enters a downtown office building. Walter, like many who aspire to enter corporate America through unskilled beginnings, is exposed to the world of Mr. Arnold and wants to be like him. But Mr. Arnold only offers Walter a newspaper. Walter lacks the education and the opportunities that would admit him into the office building that towers over him. Walter stands outside the building. He does not participate in corporate deals, he observes them with a sense of frustration.

Walter's position as a passive onlooker with frustrated dreams results in an oppositional language that explores the dynamics of the frustrated, black, male ego. His ego, having disregarded the myth of Big Walter, tells us about Mr. Arnold's myth. In Walter's attempt to measure up to Arnold, he totally neglects the survival strategies of Big Walter and the memories of Lena his mother.

Lena encourages aspiration through education and racio-familial memory; these are elements that transcend the individualistic aspirations of Walter. Unlike her son, Lena wants to devote the $10,000 insurance payment to three different purposes: education, housing, and savings. The purchase of a two-flat house represents the failed dream of Big Walter and Lena. The dream is secured but it remains the responsibility of the family to pay the mortgage. Lena says that she will use "part of the insurance money for a down payment and everybody kind of pitch in." The house is a collective sign that signifies the possibility of achieving a group aspiration. The two-flat is no mere signifier of middle-class desires for home ownership nor does it represent a desire to live in an integrated neighborhood. The new home carries forth Big Walter's dream since it connects his past struggle with the present state of the family's crowded living quarters. The house also becomes the collective sign of the Youngers' ability to resist the white Clybourne Park Improvement Association's bribe to forego their civil rights.

When Walter is entrusted with the responsibility to open the savings account for Beneatha and the checking account for himself, he gives the $6500 to Willie Harris, who absconds with the money. Walter's entrepreneurial dreams are crushed but they resurface when Mr. Lindner appears. Lindner is the representative of the Clybourne Park Improvement Association, a group of white homeowners who want to buy the two-flat from the Youngers at an inflated price. Earlier in the story, Walter had refused Lindner's offer but he now reconsiders it. After being swindled by Willie Harris, Walter asks Lindner to return to the Younger apartment because he now will accept the bribe. Lindner returns and Ruth tries to send Travis downstairs to prevent him from witnessing Walter accept the bribe. But Lena insists that Travis witness his father's actions. Lena says, "No. Travis, you stay right here. And you [Walter] make him [Travis] understand what you're doing. . . . You teach him good. Like Willie Harris taught you. You show where our five generations done come to. Go ahead son." Walter takes on the mantle of his deceased father and the five generations of Youngers. He affirms the collective memory and thereby educates the sixth generation in the resistance struggle. Walter says,

> I have worked as a chauffeur most of my life—and my wife she does domestic work in people's kitchens. So does my mother. My father . . . was a laborer most of his life. And that's my sister over there, and she's going to be a doctor. This is my son, who makes the sixth generation of our family in this country. We have thought of your offer and have decided to move into our home because my father . . . my father, he earned it.

Walter Lee's monologue articulates a collective working-class voice, a racial consciousness, and a vision of black womanhood as mothers, laborers, and soon-to-be professionals.

Raisin explores, then, three major issues: race, class, and gender. The film shows the constant friction between the laboring class of white Mr. Lindners and the equally laboring class of black Youngers. It portrays the racial and class differences between the wealthy, white Mr. Arnold, and the dreams and vision of an unskilled, black Walter Lee. It mirrors the black woman's growing awareness of her right to reject motherhood and plan parenthood around her professional career. The film celebrates the African-American vision of a collective consciousness in which polyphony reigns.

Raisin simultaneously portrays a black matriarchal family structure that is rooted in several value systems—capitalism, black feminism, religious fundamentalism, and pan-Africanism. In *Raisin,* family members discuss residential segregation, abortion, atheism, and the liberation of African nations. The presence of conflicting desires between family members and those outside the family circle permits interfamilial and extrafamilial dialogue and, simultaneously, avoids the erasure of black generative discourses.

The film industry's increasing need to attract African-American audiences requires it to create black-oriented products. But to understand this industrial necessity, one must also discern the ways in which blacks participated in the artistic construction of black-oriented films. Film industry executives, even during the period of independently-produced, studio-distributed films, such as *Take a Giant Step* and *A Raisin in the Sun,* reaffirmed the dominant visual representation of the black family. However, black screenwriters such as Peterson and Hansberry used dialogue to undermine a film's apparent middle-class values. This indeterminacy of meaning is only one of the levels at which tension occurs. Similarly, certain forms of reception can assimilate, appropriate, and resist any visual representation of black family life.

The illusory nature of dominant racial-gender discourses generated by most films helps to circumvent the threatening nature of a popularized "black" form and its reception. Consequently a subversive black character, such as Beneatha in *A Raisin in the Sun,* is unthreatening in her affirmation of black socialism. Beneatha's indeterminate reception permits the production of subversive works. Her pan-African and black feminist subjectivity refuses assimilation by a mass audience. Her dialogue on Africa, planned parenthood, and feminism invites a resistant spectatorial positioning. The indeterminate receptive quality of black family films, then, permits dominant and subversive readings.

By the seventies, the independently-produced, studio-distributed African-American family film permitted a broader vision of black American life. Black middle-class family melodramas, such as *Take a Giant*

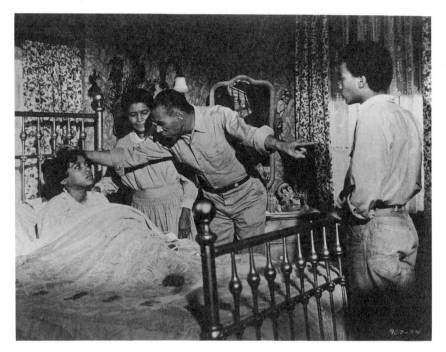

From The Learning Tree. *Courtesy of the Museum of Modern Art Film Stills Archive.*

Step and *A Raisin in the Sun,* spoke to the era of integration and polite militancy.

During this period the black film market required films that spoke to despairing urban youths, rather than to parents who remained hopeful that social programs would return. Black and white youths demanded and regularly paid the price of admission. Urban black youths frequented inner city movie theaters while white youths went to those in the suburbs. Many inner city theaters showed films that attracted a black youth audience. Consequently, black family films no longer hid the single-parent welfare family behind smiles of hope. They revealed the grim reality of urban uprisings, abandoned buildings, gang violence, and a new generation locked into economic dependency and psychological poverty. Some of the films that document this period are J. E. Franklin's screen adaptation *Black Girl,* Eric Monte's screenplay *Cooley High* (AIP, 1975), and Joseph A. Walker's screen adaptation *The River Niger.*

The hybrid black family narrative, like the hybrid minstrelsy humor of Eddie Murphy, can conceal its racist, sexist, and homophobic elements. Such an ability to conceal becomes equal to the hybrid's ability to reveal itself as one with the majority of its *imagined* audience at a particular time in history. For example, Robert Townsend's *Hollywood Shuffle* (1987) was a crossover success because of its ability to explore racial stereotypes while permitting certain audiences their racist and homophobic laughter. There are many examples of hybrid black films, and the manipulation of such discourses will be the focus of the black action film chapter.

4

Black Action Film

Modes of film production and of black spectatorship can be divided into three levels of empowerment. *Resistance* connotes any independent form that empowers black culture and the blacks who make the film. *Assimilation* describes any black version of a master text (e.g., *Shaft* and formula detective films). *Appropriation* refers to any mixture of a conventional form with black folklore such as *Super Fly* and *Sweetback,* which celebrates the gangster film and uses heroes taken from black urban street culture—the dope dealer and the pimp. Each level of empowerment is interchangeable and each is immersed in double-talk. Thus, any black-oriented film or any black viewing position, because of its dialogic nature, can repudiate racism at the same time that it accepts or resists sexism, classism, ethnocentrism, and homophobia.

One must question essentialist and totalizing terms that collapse differences to a single factor such as race or class. Any effort to represent blacks imaginatively or theoretically as a monolithic entity furthers the dehumanization of African-American life. Discussion must also focus on the socioeconomic needs of a diverse audience. Any discussion of "black" spectatorship should not be construed to advocate racial essentialism—black spectatorship describes an *imaginary* and freely accessible viewing relationship. The black spectator refers to the *lived* experiences of people of African ancestry. The black viewing position incorporates identities of gender, sexuality, ethnicity, and class. In the context of action films, black spectatorship describes how various black audiences *might* interpret blackface and hybrid and satiric hybrid subtypes of the black action film genre. Black spectatorship does not guarantee a politically correct or inaccurate viewing position.

The emergence of studio-distributed black action films corresponds to the black community's increasing rejection of nonviolent protest.[1] Black action films are a popularized version of this discontent. The way that film studios market and construct black hero(ine)s delineates how this industry deals with the desires of the African-American audience and their lived experiences. This chapter analyzes why black action film subtypes first emerged and what factors led to their demise or retention. The sociopsychic nature of black spectatorship is also discussed. In analyzing the issues of marketing and spectatorship, I describe different levels of black empowerment in the production, distribution, and reception of black action films. Using the previously discussed paradigmatic forms (blackface minstrelsy, hybrid minstrelsy, and satiric hybrid minstrelsy), I describe how certain action films reflect these narrative forms.

The hybrid black action film presents a hero who is determined by race, gender, and, to a lesser extent, by class. The hybrid subtype depicts white males as the hero's sole obstacle and the possession of white and black females as vehicles for the hero's salvation. The hybrid action narrative merely inverts the racial aspect of white patriarchy, making it a black patriarchal system.

The two subtypes represent the dualistic nature of American race and gender relations as well as the demands of American moral conventions that require that criminals never escape punishment. Ironically, black heroes escape punishment because, according to black action film conventions, blacks are the victims of a white patriarchal system. In both subtypes, black heroes have an insatiable appetite for females, material objects, and violence; this permits the narrative to gloss over a wide range of African-American life experiences.

The third subtype, satiric hybrid black action film, promotes a class-oriented hero who confronts figures of authority regardless of their race. This narrative type sometimes advances multicultural and interracial solidarity and criticizes the racial essentialism of blackface and hybrid action films, but it does little else. Satiric hybrid action films use women as vehicles for the hero's escape, and images of female empowerment are rare. Nevertheless, although the satiric subtype shares some of the misogynist and heterosexist qualities of the other two black action film subtypes, it denies a one-to-one relationship in which all blacks are good and all whites are bad. Such films as *Shaft* (1971), *Super Fly* (1972), and *Sweet Sweetback's Baadasssss Song* (1971) are examples of the three respective subtypes.

Spectators of blackface, hybrid, and satiric hybrid action films are asked to believe that racial factors are the sole determinant of poverty and that the white man is the only obstacle in the hero's (and their) path to freedom. The audience can then celebrate the hero's use of illegal and violent means to ensure his escape from impoverished conditions. Some spectators find these subtypes entertaining for all the above reasons; however, they find it ludicrous to imitate these heroes. Others resist these films and become highly critical of their effects on the black action film audience.

Before turning to the action films of the seventies, I want to discuss a transitional black action film whose narrative dramatized integrationist politics, whose production resulted from interracial collaboration, and whose marketing was limited to theatres in black communities. *A Man Called Adam* (Embassy Pictures, 1966) transcends racial dualism while it explores racial discrimination and economic exploitation in the music industry.

From Bitterness to Anger

Sammy Davis, Jr.'s production of *A Man Called Adam* features Davis as Adam Johnson, a frustrated and embittered black jazz musician. Like other black action heroes, Adam is very sexual. Adam has relationships with several black women. Unlike black action heroes of the seventies, Adam has no interracial sexual encounters, but there is one scene in which he is offered a chance to pursue such intimacy. Before dawn, Adam enters a sleazy bar and exchanges sexual innuendos with two white women who are seated at a table awaiting a paying john. The white women's interest in Adam is based on his ability to exchange money for their white flesh. Their racial and sexual presence proposes a capitalist interracial and sexual venture rather than expresses the desired outcome of the civil rights movement—racial harmony. He leaves the bar exchanging words that imply his lack of interest in their carnal proposition. Adam's heroism is established by his ability to leave these women and, later, seek a fulfilling relationship with a politically conscious black woman.

Unlike the nonviolent strategies of Martin Luther King, Adam's heroism celebrates the retaliatory violence promoted by Malcolm X. Adam does not believe in passive resistance or "putting his best foot forward," in fact, he bitterly rejects this tactic. In one scene, he punches a white police officer who verbally abused him. Later Adam's white agent, Manny, tries to discipline Adam by sending him to the South on a six-week tour. Manny callously says, "Look, you're a musician, you go down there and blow. And you get in the bus, in the back if necessary!

Now, sign these contracts or get out of my life." Adam exchanges some controlled words with his agent. He pours another glass of whiskey from his agent's bar and breaks the bottle. Then he brandishes the broken bottle and makes Manny crawl. Adam bitterly returns, "That's discipline," and walks out of Manny's office. Manny blackballs Adam from performing in New York jazz clubs. The determinate forces of the music industry, as personified in Manny, force Adam to beg Manny's forgiveness. Adam apologizes and dies a young, embittered jazz musician.

In the above two scenes Johnson violently rejected the attempts of white men who wanted to dehumanize him legally and professionally. Like the black action film protagonists who follow, Adam Johnson uses violence and anger, rather than legal action and patience, to maintain his humanity. Unlike the action hero, Adam is alienated, embittered, and an "unpoliticized" member of a black community of jazz musicians.

A Man Called Adam also presents an alternative to Adam Johnson's violent nature. Claudia, Adam's lover, is a "politicized-integrationist" college student. She participated in the southern black student sit-ins, a form of passive resistance to desegregate public places. Claudia patiently endures Adam as she endured white racism. Her character reflects the political consciousness and middle-class sensibilities of Beneatha Younger in *A Raisin in the Sun* (1961). Adam, like Walter in *Raisin,* represents the black community's impatience and its frustration with racism. *Time* magazine reported "the film's message . . . ends with the distressing thought that nonviolence, man, will get you nowhere."[2]

Between 1966 and 1974, major studio-distributed black action films generated the largest opportunities for blacks in Hollywood. *A Man Called Adam* is one of the first studio-distributed films that credits a black as one of its producers. Ike Jones, according to *Variety,* "is the first Negro to receive a producer's credit on a [major] U.S. pic." In the same article *Variety* reports that Nat King Cole planned to produce the original screenplay for *A Man Called Adam.*[3] The film's distribution was limited to movie theaters in African-American communities, a marketing strategy that major studios adopted in the 1970s for their black action films.[4]

Thus, *Adam* is a forerunner of the black action film that emphasized a black ghetto environment and a certain type of heroic protagonist. Embassy's intention to distribute the film to black urban areas reduced the estimated box-office receipts and required a low production budget. The formal and cultural elements that are dramatized in the film and Embassy Pictures' production and distribution strategy became the dominant mode of producing and distributing major studio films on African-American life. Thus, Embassy's marketing of *Adam* characterizes a *mas-*

ter discourse by which major studios market their black-oriented film fare.[5]

Black Power and Urban Revolts

The African-American community's growing impatience with white racial and social intransigence and black second-class citizenship produced two major results in the late 1960s: racial violence and black cultural nationalism. Earlier in the decade, African-Americans and white liberals had sought to dismantle racial segregation in America through nonviolent protest, a tactic designed to make whites recognize the immorality of racially discriminatory practices and thereby change these practices.[6]

Young black students at first used passive resistance in the form of sit-ins and eat-ins. Other young blacks organized voter registration drives. Their experiences with the 1963 voter registration drive in Mississippi, however, discouraged them from continuing non-violent tactics.[7] In the fall of 1963, SNCC (the Student Non-violent Coordinating Committee) helped organize a voter registration drive in Mississippi. When Mississippi authorities refused to recognize the black registrants, the blacks founded the Mississippi Freedom Democratic party (MFDP) in defiance of the regular Mississippi Democratic party.[8] The MFDP elected sixty-eight delegates, four of whom were white, from its members to represent it at the 1964 Democratic convention. Again, black Mississippians met with white intransigence, but this time it was not limited to the South. The National Democratic party refused to seat the MFDP delegation. Consequently, "The MFDP . . . and the young black leaders of SNCC, and black radicals in the country . . . read the pressure they had been subjected to by the President and the Democrats as conclusive confirmation of their emerging thesis that 'the system' was ineradicably permeated by racism. . . . The MFDP and some of its supporters, in other words, saw the Democratic Party and liberals generally, white or black, no longer as the hope of a solution, but as part of the problem."[9]

By 1967, and as a logical result of the frustrated attempts to gain first-class citizenship for blacks, many black grassroot organizations became more aggressive in their tactics. Stokeley Carmichael, who later became an advocate of retaliatory violence, was elected chairman of SNCC in 1966. At the 1966 Congress of Racial Equality (CORE) convention, the membership formally repudiated nonviolence and endorsed the slogan "Black Power."[10]

In October of 1966 the Black Panther Party for Self Defense was founded. According to Reginald Major, "The Panthers were a logical development of earlier black revolutionary programs, particularly those of Robert Williams, the [Black] Muslims, Malcolm X, and the more activist civil rights organizations such as SNCC."[11] Their shared purpose was made explicit on May 2, 1967. BPP members entered the California state capitol with M-1 rifles, 12-gauge shotguns, and .45-caliber pistols. They were protesting the Mulford Act, a pending state legislature bill to restrict the carrying of firearms. The Panthers interpreted this bill as an attempt to disarm the black community, which would then become victims of "racist police agencies throughout the country." These organizations and actions indicated a growing militancy among young blacks.

At the same time that black activists repudiated nonviolence, there was a wave of inner-city revolts. Several urban uprisings occurred in African-American communities between the Watts (Los Angeles) Rebellion on August 9, 1965, and insurrections in other cities in the spring of 1968. These urban insurrections were nationally telecast. Images of black inner-city life were formed or reinforced by the television images that portrayed blacks looting neighborhood stores while buildings burned. Destruction and the destructive seemed to define the black community. The combination of televised news coverage of the urban uprisings and the militant rhetoric of black armed resistance intensified white middle-class America's opinion of blacks as a violent people.

Most whites did not socialize with blacks, nor did their education include courses dealing with African-American socio-cultural experiences. They naively formulated their ideas about African-Americans from Anglo-American literature, television, and the movies. In March 1968, the National Advisory Commission on Civil Disorders published its report, which explained how white racism produced black inner-city violence. Thus, white Americans were further encouraged to believe that violence characterized black behavior.[12]

Young, inner-city blacks directed their frustrations toward what they called the "man's" institutions, property, and laws—"the system." Some of these blacks stressed the need to secure economic and political changes by armed overthrow of white institutions and by the creation of strong independent black institutions. Others, however, emphasized intellectual and psychological changes by developing black studies programs in institutions of higher education and by establishing black community theaters. Channeling their anger into the practice of Black Art, discussions of black aesthetics, and the development of collectives that continued black creative traditions, the proponents of black community theaters emphasized black cultural nationalism. This, of course, was not the first time blacks had advocated cultural nationalism. In 1937, Richard Wright promoted the importance of discovering black art in black culture and experience. In his seminal essay "Blueprint for Negro Writing," he wrote,

> In a folklore molded out of rigorous and inhuman conditions of life . . .
> the Negro achieved his most indigenous and complete expression. Blues,
> spirituals, and folk tales recounted from mouth to mouth; the whispered
> words of a black mother to her black daughter on the ways of men, to
> confidential wisdom of a black father to his black son; the swapping of sex
> experiences on street corners from boy to boy in the deepest vernacular;
> work songs sung under blazing suns—all these formed channels through
> which the racial wisdom flowed.[13]

Disregarding earlier campaigns for black nationalism, however, blacks of the sixties saw theirs as a new movement. In 1968, Black Arts critic and poet Larry Neal wrote that the movement's ideology stressed the importance of creating art "directed at problems within Black America . . . with the premise that there is a well defined Afro-American audience. An audience that must see itself and the world in terms of its own interests. The Black Arts Movement represents the flowering of a cultural nationalism."[14]

Almost fifty years earlier, black independent filmmaker William Foster had recognized that there was a black audience that was interested in black-oriented art. But Neal argued that the first wave of black independent filmmakers, such as Foster and other creative artists of the Negro Renaissance, "did not address . . . [themselves] to the mythology and the life styles of the Black community."[15]

This new wave of black creative activity, which arose from the ashes of riot-torn ghettos, rejected art that appealed to white America's aesthetic morality. Neal, using the words of Etheridge Knight, wrote, "Any Black man who masters the technique of his particular art form, [but] who adheres to the white aesthetic, and who directs his work towards a white audience is, in one sense, protesting."[16] Neal, like others, felt that "protest" was outdated and ineffectual. The Black Arts critics demanded the use of black-oriented criteria to assess the artistic value of creative works; they called this process a fundamental principle of the black aesthetic.[17] As Neal writes, "Unless the Black artist establishes a 'Black Aesthetic' he [or she] will have no future at all. To accept the white aesthetic is to accept and validate a society that will not allow him [or her] to live. The Black artist must create new forms . . . values . . . and along with other Black authorities, [s]he must create new history . . . symbols, myths and . . . must be accountable for it only to the Black people."[18]

Having established that there was a young black audience receptive to thoughts about violence, it should have been possible to create black action films that appealed to this audience while satisfying a black aesthetic. The studio-distributed black action films of the 1970s, however, never reached this ideal for two reasons: either because they were not independent productions, or because black independent producers had to rely on major distributors.

Harold Cruse had warned about the difficulties that black cultural nationalists who attempted to create according to a black aesthetic might experience in maintaining their autonomy. He wrote in 1967, "The political activists will attempt to either suppress or control the creative elements, and especially the writers. . . . The Negro writer, who is nationalistically oriented, must, at all times, fight within movements to maintain his creative and critical independence within a reasonable context of the general aims of the movement."[19]

The validity of Cruse's warning concerning efforts by black political activists to control black creativity in filmmaking will be discussed later. But it is also important to understand how white filmmakers and major studios control black images either by manipulating the blacks who create those images or by producing their own spurious images. This control can be seen in two prototypical black action films that major studios distributed or produced during the 1970s.

Melvin Van Peebles's *Sweet Sweetback's Baadasssss Song* was a popular black action film that dramatized the experiences of an inarticulate, black male hustler called Sweetback. He was reared as a sexual performer in a Los Angeles brothel and, as a child, was given the name "Sweetback" by a prostitute who admired his sexual skill.

The major conflict evolves when Sweetback is falsely arrested and taken from the brothel by two white detectives. While the detectives are taking Sweetback to the police station, they arrest and beat a young black militant name Moo Moo; Sweetback intervenes and brutally attacks the detectives. Consequently, Sweetback must flee the Los Angeles police and a sheriff's posse with bloodhounds. In addition, he must cross the desert and enter Mexico to gain his safety. The film concludes with a promise of Sweetback's vengeful return.

Sweetback was the first black action film that attracted large, black, teenage audiences, which was the intent of Van Peebles who had decided to make a film for the "unpoliticized" black filmgoer. He "wanted a victorious film. A film where niggers could walk out standing tall instead of avoiding each other's eyes, looking once again like they'd had it."[20]

Van Peebles consciously avoided a "politicized" film because he wanted to reach a large ready-made audience. "The film simply couldn't be a didactic discourse," he wrote, "which would end up playing (if I could find a distributor) to an empty theater except for ten or twenty aware brothers who would pat me on the back and say it tells it like it is."[21] Van Peebles rationalized his rejection of "didactic discourse" films by saying that he wanted to entertain and instruct the black audience whom he calls "Brer" (brother): "If Brer is bored, he's bored. One of the problems we must face squarely is that to attract the mass we have to produce work that not only instructs but entertains."[22] A large group of unpoliticized Brers did, in fact, support his film at the box office.

The Making of a Hero Called Sweetback

Because black popular audiences were starving for black heroes who were not made for white audiences, Van Peebles attempted to answer this need and make a financial profit. In creating a new black hero, he drew from both white popular culture and black mythology and folklore. He used some heroic elements that mainstream culture had popularized in such films as Clint Eastwood westerns. In those works the film heroes tend to be social outcasts, tight-lipped, single males who are placed in violent situations. For example, Eastwood in *Hang 'em High* (1968) portrayed an inarticulate gunfighter who survived his own hanging and sought vengeance against the nine men who hanged him.

Van Peebles also used elements from the mythic street hero of urban black folklore—one skilled in fighting, performing sexually, and evading the police. Unlike most white heroes of the action film genre, Sweetback participates in sex primarily to survive, and he performs with both white and black women. For example, when Sweetback is running from the police, he is sexually challenged by a former black lover who refuses to help him unless he makes love to her. Much later, he and Moo Moo are captured by a white motorcycle gang who delivers them to the gang's leader, a husky white female. The leader challenges Sweetback to a duel and allows him to select his weapon. Sweetback, who has been reared in a brothel, pragmatically chooses sex. Like the black prostitute before her, the white gang leader admires Sweetback's sexual agility and so gives Sweetback and Moo Moo their freedom. In these sexual feats, Sweetback becomes a black urban folk hero as the dispassionate stud; that is, he gives his two female adversaries sexual pleasure without showing an iota of self-enjoyment. His ability to perform skillfully requires the discipline of a soldier intent upon killing the enemy; such a performance cannot be interpreted as primitive lust nor a reflection of emotional desire.

Furthermore, like Staggerlee and other mythic urban heroes, Sweetback directs violence against unjust white authority figures. For example, when Sweetback witnesses the detectives beating Moo Moo, he immediately identifies the enemy and violently attacks the two detectives. In a later scene, several white police officers enter Sweetback's hideout, where the hero gives a repeat performance without any show of personal enjoyment of the violence.

Both Sweetback's disinterested and skilled sexuality and controlled and motivated violence are necessary for his escape. Earlier film images of black men had never been presented like Sweetback because the master race narrative viewed empowered black men as studs. According to the master text, black male sexuality was animalistic and instinctively violent. Thus, when Van Peebles resisted the master text and created Sweetback with a controlled and motivated violence, Van Peebles's heroic idea seemed revolutionary to certain members of the black community.

This new black hero contrasted with previous black male heroes who were created by white and black writers of earlier periods. Before *Sweetback,* white writers and filmmakers created stories and images that psychologically, physically, and sexually castrated black men or, for example, in D. W. Griffith's *Birth of a Nation* (1915), depicted black men as brutal primitives driven by an innate desire for violence and for sex with white women.

Van Peebles also rejected the white-oriented "black-as-martyr" heroes created by earlier writers. In these films, which were popular after World War II, the black heroes often died in ways intended to promote racial integration, or else were saved by benevolent whites. The earliest examples of such films appear in a postwar "problem film" cycle: *Home of the Brave* (Kramer, 1949) dramatizes the problem of integrating a black soldier named Moss into an all-white army unit. Moss becomes the victim of racial slurs and consequently suffers a psychological illness, from which he is cured by a white doctor. *Intruder in the Dust* (MGM, 1949) presents a white southern lawyer who successfully defends a black southerner falsely accused of murdering a white man and threatened with lynching. *No Way Out* (Twentieth Century–Fox, 1950) depicts a northern black doctor accused of malpractice that led to the death of his patient. Ultimately, he is cleared by a white hospital administrator. Even though white screenwriters of the sixties introduced stronger black heroes, they often deprived their heroes of some qualities identified with urban blacks. For example, in the action film *In the Heat of the Night* (UA, 1967), black New York police detective Virgil Tibbs is not a victim, but he is portrayed in an asexual guise.

Sweetback was popular because black inner-city youths and black street people identified with the film's imaginative reflection of their real lives, which were ignored by Hollywood. There had been too many real martyrs, but white films never told of the brutality that America inflicted upon Medgar Evers, Martin Luther King, Jr., Malcolm X, and countless less famous young blacks who died from police beatings, a form of racial lynching. Many black inner-city youths who had participated in urban revolts were attracted to the heroic aspects of Sweetback. The film's portrayal of the black ghetto and the villains who prey on it seemed to express the socio-cultural reality understood by many streetwise young black men who identified with values outside the rules of the law and courts and the morality of the church.

Van Peebles made villains of both black and white police detectives and those who cooperate with them. For example, a white police official publicly calls blacks "niggers," even though, later, he privately apologizes to a black detective. The film also presents a member of the street community as a black villain. The brothel owner Beatle first hands Sweetback over to two white detectives. After Sweetback escapes, Beatle again informs the police of Sweetback's whereabouts. The film also shows the falsity of black preachers who prey on the weaknesses of their congregations. For example, a black preacher supplies women for Beatle's brothel and tells Sweetback, "Ain't it strange how our folks rejoice when we die. . . . They believe that maybe it will be better on the other side. It's my job to make them believe that it's true."[23] The images of the police, the brothel keeper, and the black preacher all seem to reflect what Richard Wright called the "rigorous and inhuman conditions of life." The film reflected social conditions that black street people instantly recognized. This audience can be defined as a street-oriented film culture.[24]

Black inner-city youths who supported Sweetback became an important market for black action films. Between 1969 and 1971, 74 percent of American moviegoers were under thirty years of age according to a survey cited in the 13 October 1971 issue of Variety. Hence, producers needed to appeal to a youthful audience. But black youth, of course, represented an even more specific group of youths to whom producers needed to direct their work. The fact that Sweetback's domestic theatrical rentals amounted to $4,100,000 indicates that producers could make significant profits by creating black action films for young blacks.[25]

Not all segments of the black population approved of Sweet Sweetback's Baadasssss Song, however. The film was criticized both by black cultural nationalists who wanted explicitly politicized black films and by other blacks who wanted films in which blacks were identified with middle-class values. These two groups tended to be Van Peebles's most ardent critics. They argued that his film exploited the tawdry underbelly of black street life. In addition, they argued that he avoided dramatizing the socioeconomic causes that had produced the moral decadence.

Most of the criticism was directed at the film's portrayal of black

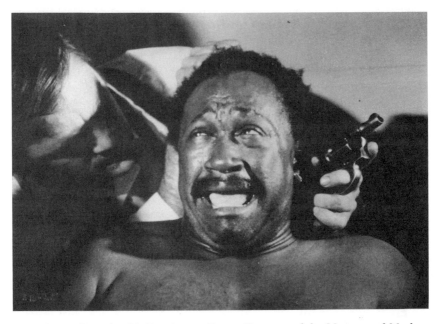

From Sweet Sweetback's Baadasssss Song. *Courtesy of the Museum of Modern Art Film Stills Archive.*

women.[26] For example, the opening scene takes place in the kitchen of a brothel where a young boy eats while black prostitutes watch him lustfully. In the next scene, a prostitute bids the boy to enter her room and makes love with him. These two scenes were interpreted differently by two important black socio-cultural representatives. Black Panther party minister of defense Huey P. Newton, who represented a street-oriented but politicized perspective, wrote, "The music indicates that this is not a sexual scene, this is a very sacred rite. For the boy, who was nourished to health, is now being baptized into manhood; and the act of love, the giving of manhood, is also bestowing upon the boy the characteristics which will deliver him from very difficult situations. People who look upon this as a sex scene miss the point completely, and people who look upon the movie as a sex movie miss the entire message of the film."[27] Here, Newton articulates the street ethics of manhood which equates sexuality with a form of masculine political power. But, according to Newton's reasoning, black women are mere intermediaries who are absent of any political deliverance through such a sexual exchange. Newton's analysis reflects the misogynist conventions that blackface, hybrid, and satirical hybrid action films celebrate.

Consequently, in a pamphlet entitled "From a Black Perspective" Chi-

Advertisement for Sweet Sweetback's Baadasssss Song. *Courtesy of Cinemation Industries/Melvin Van Peebles.*

cago's Kuumba Workshop, a black cultural nationalist drama group, rejected Newton's male-oriented interpretation.[28] A member of Kuumba wrote, "Newton . . . seriously mistakes Van Peebles' use of sex. Newton argues . . . that the opening scene . . . is not really sexual, but spiritual and tender. The scene opens with four black prostitutes voraciously peering down at a young black boy eating, and then a filthy, graphic look at one of the whores engaged in sexual intercourse with the boy."[29] The pamphlet also denied that Van Peebles used sex "as a spiritual force as Newton argues" but insisted instead that he presented nude scenes "to arouse and give his audience a vicarious thrill."[30] Kuumba did not deny the possibility of portraying black sensuality as spiritual. It argued that this film fell short of such a portrait.

Sweetback did not try to educate its black audience for liberation. As the representative of Kuumba stated, "In terms of black aesthetic,

Sweetback failed an essential principle—that black art must be functional. Black art must do more than merely stimulate. It must educate, provide a deeper understanding of black people and the forces shaping their lives and the lives of others, critically examine society, and ultimately enlist blacks in the struggle for their liberation."[31] Kuumba's criticisms reflect a value system that is generated by both a politicized black diasporic cultural memory (black cultural nationalism) and the belief that illicit sexual relationships dehumanize rather than liberate the black community.[32] Probably no other black director has provoked such critical controversy since Micheaux angered parts of the black community with *The Brute* (1920) and *The Symbol of the Unconquered* (1920). Even the popularity of *Sweetback* worried critics who feared that young blacks would model their behavior after the film's portrayal of black sexuality and relatiatory violence. Here I disagree with their conclusions, since viewing relationships are imaginary and tend to dissipate as one walks further from the movie seat. Like any other spectators, blacks can either assimilate and appropriate, or resist racist and misogynist fantasies—all of these possible moves keep them afloat in stormy waters.

There was a middle point between Newton's high praise and the Kuumba Workshop's denunciation. On the one hand, blacks who find psychological satisfaction in films featuring violent black heroes have just as much right to have their tastes satisfied as do whites who find pleasure in white heroes such as Clint Eastwood and Charles Bronson. If Hollywood refuses to create virile black heroes, a black filmmaker should not be condemned for attempting to fill the void. On the other hand all filmmakers, white or black, can be criticized if they demean one sex or the other. It is inappropriate for *Sweetback* to include positive images of male homosexuals and Mexican males, both of whom help Sweetback escape from white policemen, while the film lacks any dignified portrayal of black women.

Although *Sweetback* was independently produced by a black, I do not consider it a black independent film. It was distributed by Jerry Gross's Cinemation Industries, a mini-major distribution company and the parent company of Cinecom Theatres.[33] Cinemation distributed and produced such popular low-budget porn films as *Inga* (1968) and *Fanny Hill* (1969). One reason for Cinemation's interest in Van Peebles's film was the erotic portrayal of women, a major emphasis of their own low-budget films. Anticipating such a reaction, Van Peebles intensified the eroticism of his film in order to make it appeal to Cinemation.

This distinction between independent distribution and distribution by major or mini-major companies is significant to any analysis of black independent film because black filmmakers may alter their scripts to aim for distribution by major studios. Van Peebles probably altered his film in several ways to aim for major distribution, since he hoped that his film would "be able to sustain itself as a viable commercial product." He writes, "The [white] Man . . . might go along with you if at least there is some bread in it for him. But he ain't about to go carrying no messages for you, especially a relevant one for free."[34] Even though he realized that he would have to satisfy Cinemation's tastes, Van Peebles undoubtedly gained for *Sweetback* more visibility and more bookings in theaters throughout the nation and took in more money than if he had depended on nonprofit distribution organizations.[35]

The Studio-Produced Black Action Film

Concurrent with the independent production of *Sweetback,* Metro–Goldwyn Mayer made a late entry into the black film market with its production of the very popular black detective film *Shaft.*[36] *Shaft* was directed by Gordon Parks, Hugh A. Robertson was the editor, and Isaac Hayes composed the music; all three men are African-Americans. But *Shaft*'s scenarist Ernest Tidyman, producer Joel Freeman, and executive producers Sterling Silliphant and Roger Lewis are whites, and they controlled the most essential aspects of production. Hence, *Shaft* is representative of a black action film produced by a major studio,[37] and a look at *Shaft*'s production reveals how a major studio packages a particular black action film to appeal to a black popular audience. Particularity is significant here, for according to sociologist Garth Jowett, "Popular culture functions in a much smaller social unit, and any given society can, in fact, have a large number of coexisting popular cultures . . . at any one time."[38] *Shaft* appealed to a particular mass audience whom I call a black popular, or unpoliticized, audience.[39] This viewing relationship is one of assimilation, but other relationships are also present. For example, a white male viewer might enjoy the sex and violence and ignore the racial factor; this spectatorial position characterizes the appropriation mode. Viewers who adopted the resistance mode would reject the entire concept of a black detective while they assimilate sexist and violent imagery. There also exists polyphony in all three receptive modes which permits openings of free zones where resistance can assimilate (as in "I hated the picture but after thinking about that scene, I think I like it").

In order to appeal to this audience MGM recognized its need to employ a black-oriented advertising firm, one experienced in attracting a black popular audience. MGM hired UniWorld, which popularized *Shaft* by using the rhetoric of black power. This rhetoric was most apparent in how UniWorld described the hero and the black artists who participated

in *Shaft*'s production. For example, *Variety* reported UniWorld's advertisement description of the protagonist John Shaft as, "A lone, black
Superspade—a man of flair and flamboyance who has fun at the expense
of the (white) establishment." Then Byron Lewis, the president of
UniWorld, told *Variety* that his agency created "a code" that the black
community understood. He admitted that his black agency's advertising
exploited the fantasies of the black community: "Mention of the Mob . . .
gets across the idea of the numbers—a significant part of black life. . . .
the fantasy that control of the numbers can be taken away from the
Mafia—a totally unrealistic idea at present, but one that establishes Shaft
as a guy who beat the system."[40] UniWorld did not limit its task to creating
a "Superspade" image. The agency also emphasized "the behind-the-
camera participation of blacks," thereby appealing to blacks who would
appreciate the film as a black production or could fantasize that blacks
had somehow beat the Hollywood system and taken over Metro–
Goldwyn Mayer studios.[41]

Despite this obvious effort to attract a black popular audience by
means of calculated rhetoric and images MGM, like other major studios, invested black heroes with mainstream values. In doing so, it did
not create mythic black heroes. Instead, like the doll-makers who
painted Barbie's face brown, MGM merely created black-skinned repli-
cas of the white heroes of action films. A textual analysis of *Shaft* provides evidence of such weaknesses in a black action film written, produced, and distributed by white studios.

Harlem crime boss Bumpy Jones hires black private detective John
Shaft to rescue Bumpy's kidnapped daughter, whom the Mafia wants to
exchange for control of Bumpy's crime organization. The police fear
that this conflict between two crime families might erupt into a race riot
because the situation pits white and black criminals against each other.
Shaft and a group of Harlem militants rescue Bumpy's daughter; Harlem crime thereby remains in the hands of a black man, and a potential
urban uprising is avoided.

The film does not promote the same heroic values that *Sweetback*
dramatized. Shaft works within a white system (he's a detective sanctioned by white authorities). Even though he retains a keen knowledge of
Harlem street life, he also lives in Greenwich Village and has a midtown
office. He never socializes with Harlemites. Instead, he is a habitué of an
integrated Greenwich Village bar. His knowledge of Harlem and resi-
dence in the Village suggests that he has somehow bettered himself without forfeiting his ghetto savoir faire. Shaft's sole confidants, a white police
detective and a black middle-class family, reflect his distance from the
Harlem street community. The white writers thus created a black suffi-
ciently knowledgeable about black street life that he can fit into it, but

From Shaft. *Courtesy of the Museum of Modern Art Film Stills Archive.*

tore him from those roots and placed him only in white and black middle-class settings. The implication is that the wise black will want to sever ties with the people of Harlem and find a place among whites. This idea is confirmed by the fact that the white writers depict the residents of Harlem as though they were primarily militants or gangsters.

In contrast to Sweetback, who rebelled against authority figures, Shaft and other black gangsters fight only against those outside the law—black gangsters and Italian hoods. Shaft may defy his Italian-American police-detective friend verbally, but he never allows such defiance to take a physical form. Thus Shaft, supposedly a black hero, is characterized as one who swaggers belligerently among white and black men, knows Harlem but lives and works outside it, is a close friend only to a black middle-class family and an Italian-American police detective, and makes love with both white and black women.

Obviously Shaft's characteristics are quite different from those of Sweetback. Sweetback warred against an inhumane socioeconomic environment; Shaft, without motivation, verbally challenges both white and black men in an unnecessary display of toughness. Sweetback uses sex as a bodily function, an economic necessity, and a weapon for survival. Shaft and Sweetback perform sexually in ways intended to arouse the

fantasies of male viewers, but Sweetback's world is limited to black
street life; Shaft occasionally works within this circle so he can afford to
escape into an integrated middle-class social environment. In short,
Shaft's image as a black hero upholds a middle-class, raceless value
system. Clayton Riley, a black *New York Times* critic, wrote, "Inevita-
bly, 'Shaft' will be compared to the title character in Melvin Van Peebles'
cinematic triumph 'Sweet Sweetback's Baadasssss Song.' That argument
is already settled for me: 'Sweetback' wins in a walk. Which is whether
you believe a painful truth (Sweetback) is more valuable than a soothing
falsehood (Shaft)."[42]

Shaft's rentals amounted to $6,100,000 and the film cost only
$1,125,000 to produce. The profitability of this film convinced MGM to
produce two sequels, *Shaft's Big Score* (1972) and *Shaft in Africa* (1973).
The sequels were not financial successes; perhaps the black James Bond
gimmick now bored black audiences.[43]

Most studio-distributed black action films created angry, outspoken
black heroes who were outlaws or who worked in law enforcement roles.
Generally, these black action films followed one of two distinct narrative
formulas: one placed a black urban street-hero like Sweetback in a plot
that dramatized escape from white and black authority figures, and the
other portrayed a black middle-class hero like Shaft in a plot that con-
cealed police brutality and revealed interracial violence among criminals. In either scenario, the film reaches its climax with symbolic destruction of white institutions that formerly oppressed the hero. Ironically,
these two plots were mere opposites of each other, since Shaft is similar
to a policeman and Sweetback is an outlaw.

The action film subtypes, blackface, and hybrid minstrelsy rarely feature black women as heroines, but there were important exceptions.
Incorporating the racial dualism, explicit sexuality, and vengeful violence
of the black action films *Shaft* and *Sweetback,* a few studios produced
films that featured black action-oriented heroines. The most successful
attempts were made by Warner Brothers and American International.

The first of two Warner films, *Cleopatra Jones* (1973), was written by
the black actor Max Julien. The film starred fashion model Tamara
Dobson as Cleopatra Jones, a CIA narcotics agent pitted against a white
lesbian who controls the drug trade in a black community. The white-
authored sequel, *Cleopatra Jones and the Casino of Gold* (1974), sent
Cleo to Hong Kong where she destroys a Chinese, female-headed drug
ring. In both films black men assist Cleo to defeat female drug dealers.
American International produced *Coffy* (1973), *Foxy Brown* (1974), and
Friday Foster (1977), all of which featured Pam Grier in roles that person-
alize her vengeance against drug dealers, murderers, and a conniving
black lover. Grier's performances are endowed with a violent sensuality.

From Cleopatra Jones. *Courtesy of the Museum of Modern Art Film Stills Archive.*

As Coffy, Foxy, and Friday, Grier is a physically threatening but sexually appealing Amazon.

The Warner and American International films are made to engage male fantasies. Both Dobson and Grier have svelte, athletic bodies that are as thinly clad as their sisters in most action film fare. The semi-nudity of both heroines de-emphasizes their ability to physically ward off villains.

Psychologically, the five films appeal to a male ego that has been threatened by the rise of the women's liberation movement. The films are equally appealing to women who waffle between liberation and the maintenance of subservient roles. One can speculate that most audiences consider these unsheathed Amazons as objects to be sexually and racially disempowered. The penetrating male heterosexist gaze does more to disarm these heroines than their actions do to empower the filmic image of black women. In addition, Cleopatra Jones's empowerment derives from battles with women, the antithesis of truly feminist struggle. True, Coffy, Foxy, and Friday defeat men but each heroine returns to her man. None of the five films portray female solidarity, and this absence mirrors the patriarchal and heterosexist social order of most black action films.

The *Cleopatra Jones* films lessen the importance of female self-actualization, since black men physically assist the heroine and thereby diminish her power. This is not true for the *Coffy, Foxy,* or *Friday* films. The major difference between the heroines lies in the functional relationship they have to "authorized" institutions of law and order. This relationship reflects the type of audience the studio wanted to attract. The Warner films, especially the sequel that separates the black community from its heroine, present a law enforcement officer with middle-class respectability, not unlike the blackface subtype *Shaft.* The three American International films valorize sex and retaliatory violence. Just as in the satiric hybrid subtype *Sweetback,* the action heroine comes from within the black community (a folk heroine) and strikes out against her black and white male enemies. The urban youth audience for *Sweetback* and the audience of the *Coffy, Foxy,* and *Friday* films share the heroine's frustration with the slow and sometimes unfair process of law and order.

Eventually, the popularity of *Sweetback* and *Shaft* persuaded major studios to produce more black action films and give directing opportunities to blacks. Studios at first used black directors who had already directed a studio production. For example, Gordon Parks directed *The Learning Tree* (Warner, 1969), a family film; later, MGM hired him to direct *Shaft* and its sequel *Shaft's Big Score.* Bill Crain, an experienced television director, directed three black horror films: *Blacula* (AIP, 1972), *Dr. Black, Mr. Hyde* (Dimensions, 1976), and *The Watts Monster* (Dimensions, 1979). Ivan Dixon, who was a regular on the television series *Hogan's Heroes* and had directed for television, directed *Trouble Man* (Twentieth Century–Fox, 1972), a black private detective film written by a white. Dixon then directed and coproduced *The Spook Who Sat by the Door* (UA, 1973), which dramatized black urban guerilla warfare.

There were, however, exceptions to this practice. For example, Hollywood film editor Hugh A. Robertson directed *Melinda* (MGM, 1972), a

From Friday Foster. *Courtesy of the Museum of Modern Art Film Stills Archive.*

film about a black disc jockey avenging the murder of his girl friend by the syndicate. Even though Robertson had received an Academy Award nomination for film editing, he had never before directed a film.[44] Gordon Parks, Jr., whose father had taught him the trade, directed *Super Fly,* a film about a cocaine dealer; *Three the Hard Way* (Allied Artists, 1973), a film about three black men who combat white attempts at black genocide in three cities; and *Thomasine and Bushrod* (Columbia, 1974), a western that featured a black couple on a crime spree.

Some black actors were also employed to direct studio-produced black action films. For example, Sidney Poitier directed the black western *Buck and the Preacher* (Columbia, 1972), one of the first studio-

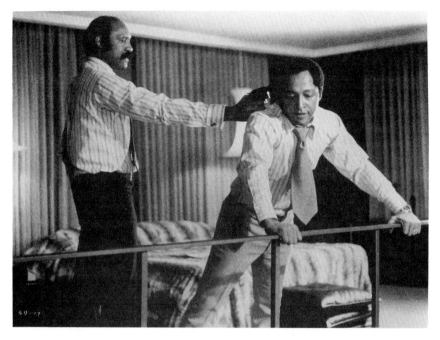

From The Spook Who Sat by the Door. *Courtesy of the Museum of Modern Art Film Stills Archive.*

produced westerns that dramatized violent black resistance to an oppressive white system.[45] Raymond St. Jacques directed, produced, and starred in *The Book of Numbers* (Avco-Embassy, 1973), a film about the numbers racket in 1930s Arkansas. Ron O'Neal, who had been featured in *Super Fly,* directed and starred in *Super Fly T.N.T.* (Paramount, 1973).

Black filmgoers, unaware that black directors in Hollywood did not have complete control of their productions, usually assumed that black directors determined how African-American life was reflected in their films. Consequently, even though some blacks were proud when any black was named director, others criticized black directors if the film did not satisfy their hopes for positive representations of black life. Black cultural nationalists and blacks who espoused middle-class values were the most adamant critics of Hollywood-produced black action films.

Nevertheless, for a period of three years black action films proved to be a popular genre that focused on black themes and provided opportunities for blacks in the American film industry. In addition, "It seemed clear by 1974 . . . that the 'blaxploitation' film [which I refer to as black action film] had just about run its course. During 1973, *Shaft in America*

(MGM), *Super Fly T.N.T.* (Warners), and *The Soul of Nigger Charley* (a Larry Spangler production) all failed to live up to expectations at the box office. . . . Producers began to recognize that those [Hollywood] films that maintained their popularity, such as *Sounder* or *Lady Sings the Blues,* had to have at least some appeal for white audiences."[46] To make black-oriented films appeal to white audiences, the studios returned to the blackface narrative form and softened hybrid and satiric hybrid black action films by pairing the black hero(ine) and a white.

Films such as *48 Hours* (Paramount, 1982), *Beverly Hills Cop* (Paramount, 1984), *Burglar* (Warner, 1987), and, to a lesser extent, *Action Jackson* (Lorimar, 1988) are versions of the blackface minstrelsy subtype that dominated the 1980s action film form. The Reagan era promoted a conservative domestic politics that equated civil rights legislation and reverse racism. Just as the Reagan administration abandoned the inner-city, major film studios overlooked the desires of black inner-city youths. Popularized versions of black empowerment were whitened in blackface. Consequently, studio-distributed hybrid action films as well as the satiric hybrid action subtype have disappeared from the screen. Instead, the African-American's emphatic speech has taken shape in the invective and lewd lyrics of black urban rappers, in black urban folk films such as Spike Lee's *Do the Right Thing* (1989), and intermittently on Arsenio Hall's televised talk show.

5

Black Comedy on the Verge of a Genre Breakdown

African-American folk humor, like most ethnic and or racial humor, has its source in the sociocultural experiences of a segregated people. This folk humor is expressed through speech and gestures that establish certain forms and ideological contents. "There is, in other words, a relationship between the group's social and economic position and the humor the group creates."[1] Since African-Americans historically have been socially segregated, at least up until the late sixties, black folk humor might not be easily understood by most nonblacks, for "the humor is based upon many intimate associations and allusions that are part of the group's social experience. The group purposely makes the humor obscure by using idioms and experiences which are unfamiliar to outsiders. For example, even if the humor should be heard outside the group, the uninitiated would need translations."[2]

Black folk humor is heard wherever African-Americans congregate: in the public spheres of the streets, the bars, and the barber shop, in the more formal context of black vaudeville, and in white settings where blacks work, often in service occupations. These racially segregated social places have allowed would-be black comedians opportunities "to introduce and refine comedy routines that relied solely on the black comic tradition. . . . Routines and jokes, for the most part, were written and developed for and depended upon the tacit understanding of the underlying assumptions and attitudes of the largely homogeneous Black audience before whom . . . [black comedians] performed."[3] This element of African-American humor has rarely dominated the commercial radio or television shows or commercial films, which have been intended for a predominantly white audience.

Urban black folk comedy (also called "black comedy") refers to any black-oriented comedy whose laughter is not evoked through an objectified *racial* other but might objectify other groups, such as women, homosexuals, and certain social classes, within and outside this community. In black comedy, laughter rises from an *inventive* narrative structure that does not retain the racially tendentious quality of blackface, hybrid, and satiric hybrid minstrel forms. Filmic examples of urban black folk comedy are Spike Lee's *She's Gotta Have It* (Island Pictures, 1986), *School Daze* (Columbia, 1988), and *Do the Right Thing* (Universal, 1989). Other examples of urban black comedies include Charles Lane's *Sidewalk Stories* (Island Pictures, 1989) and Reginald Hudlin's *House Party* (New Line Cinema, 1990). The black urban folk comedy subtype is *selectively* oppositional because its narrative structure resists both the assimilation and the negotiation of racial stereotypes. Many black urban comedy films, such as *She's Gotta Have It* and *School Daze,* however, include misogynist and homophobic elements that perpetuate derisive forms of black subjectivity. This chapter discusses and critically analyzes how the black experience is portrayed in three urban folk comedies by Lee, the most prolific director-writer-producer of studio-distributed black film.

In analyzing Lee's films, I argue against the assumption that a black director, even with final-cut privileges, can guarantee a re-vision of the filmic image of black womanhood in particular and the black experience in general. I would no more make such an argument than I would say "black" Supreme Court justice Clarence Thomas is the ideological equal of "black" former Supreme Court justice Thurgood Marshall. The purpose of this chapter is to reinforce prior discussions of the socioeconomic and sociopsychic factors (as opposed to racial and biological traits) that determine the imaginative construction of African-American life in studio-distributed black-directed films. As stated in the introduction, my argument might seem simplistic to readers who point to my bias toward independent film. Yet it is immoral for such readers to ignore the historical determinate character of masculinist, heterosexist, and racist narratives which precedes and, on occasion, consumes them. The use of critical tools to explain ruptures in these dominant narratives will be continually balanced by both a historical materialist approach and a sociopsychic analysis of the ambiguous and changeable nature of reception. I do not apologize for my belief that American popular culture (both European- and African-American) promotes middle-class individualism and valorizes racist and sexist imagery.

She's Gotta Have It typifies the urbanized black comedy film in which the absence of white characters prevents the film from reflecting a racially dualistic world. This absence also permits the film to focus on intraracial gender relations. *She's Gotta Have It* has a dualistic structure that celebrates patriarchy and heterosexuality, but neither whites nor blacks are tendentiously objectified for the benefit of a racial other. Again, the tendentious joke requires an architect who gains audience approval by objectifying a group or a representative of this group, and an audience who is amused by the architect's vilification of the chosen group or individual.

She's Gotta Have It

She's Gotta Have It is a denigrating portrait of black womanhood yet differs from previously discussed black-oriented comedies, which vilify all blacks. The female protagonist Nola Darling has three male lovers: Jamie Overstreet, Mars Blackmon, and Greer Childs. Throughout the film, each of Nola's lovers tries to force her into a monogamous relationship. Nola successfully rejects monogamy but is verbally, sexually, and psychologically abused before she acquires the fortitude to dismiss the three men. In a series of unrelated shots, Nola is constructed through discussions and actions by black women. First, Clorinda Bradford, Nola's former roommate, confesses that Nola's promiscuity led to their falling out as roommates.[4] Next, Opal Gilstrap, Nola's lesbian friend, attempts a sexual encounter that Nola politely rejects. The film thereby establishes Nola's promiscuity and heterosexuality through the speech and acts of women. Men, however, determine her sanity. Greer tells Nola, "I think you're sick. I'm not saying you're a nympho, a slut, or a whore but maybe a sex addict" (*Gotta,* 321). After digesting these words, Nola visits Dr. Clara Jamison, a sex therapist and expert on the sexuality of black women. Dr. Jamison reassures the audience that Nola is a healthy woman and that Greer is mistaken. "Some types of excessive sexual activity have all the signals of an addiction and can be treated in a fashion similar to other addictions. . . . Your friend confuses a strong healthy sex drive with sickness" (*Gotta,* 323). Unfortunately, Dr. Jamison's appraisal does not erase or balance the injurious criticisms that all three of her male lovers direct at her. The tendentious quality of *She's Gotta Have It* lies in its misogynist construction of Nola which reinforces derisive forms of black female subjectivity—her lovers commonly refer to her as a "freak" (*Gotta,* 290, 348). Although the comments of her male lovers reflect each one's inability to totally possess Nola, their insensitivity drives Nola to seek the counsel of a psychoanalyst to reassure herself of her sanity. Nola's gender-related victimization affects her psychologically, but later she will suffer physical abuse by one of her lovers. One should not underestimate the psychological and physical power of patriarchy regardless of Nola's ability to resist this oppressive force.

Nola, a single woman, attempts to define her sexuality by resisting the androcentric voices of monogamy and patriarchy. Her attempts fail because the film presents Nola as a motherless child; in fact, Nola's mother is physically and spiritually absent from the film. Furthermore, the film provides Nola with neither a sustaining relationship with women nor a platonic relationship with men. Sex defines her and circumscribes her interaction with men and her problem with women. Nola Darling cannot re-present a black feminist consciousness that celebrates liberal sexuality because Nola neither resists the collective male voices that berate her, nor refuses their desires to imbibe in her carnal pleasures. She is a slave in their rhythms.

Psychologically speaking, Jamie, Mars, and Greer occupy Nola's loft and jockey for control over her mind and body. The montage sequence of the group rape of Nola permits Jamie, her most mannerly lover, to humiliate her followed by Greer and Mars. The dialogue between Jamie and Nola illustrates their colonizer-colonized relationship, which is based on male dominance and female subservience. Jamie ends the rape, with the question, "Whose pussy is this?" and Nola meekly responds, "It's yours" (*Gotta*, 349–350), a summary of Nola's enslaved relationship with all three lovers. In commenting on the function of sex in the rape of Nola and in a similar forced sex scene in *School Daze*, Lee writes,

> I guess I can draw a comparison between *She's Gotta Have It* and *School Daze* in that it's a sexual act that transforms things; it's the kicker that puts the final thing in motion. In *She's Gotta Have It*, it's Jamie's rape of Nola, and in *School Daze* it's . . . Dap finding out that Julian [Jane's lover] coerced Jane into going to bed with Half Pint [a pledging member of Julian's fraternity].[5]

If urban folk humor has its initial source in the sociocultural experiences of the African-American people, then according to Lee, *She's Gotta Have It* and *School Daze* might be viewed as dramatizations of a black woman's dehumanizing experience with certain types of black men. But Lee has inadequately constructed Nola as an independent woman. Her possession of a loft and her requirement that sex be performed solely in her "loving bed" are not forms of independence any more than a brothel secures the independence of the prostitutes it houses—patriarchy determines the exchange of money and women.

Nola's loft is more like a game room where she meets Jamie, Mars,

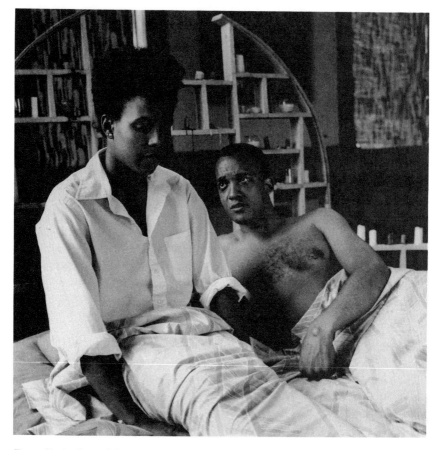

From She's Gotta Have It. *Courtesy of Pacific Film Archive.*

and Greer. Her candle-adorned "loving bed" resembles a billiard table on which Nola is the eight ball that is pocketed after the other balls have been discarded. Nola's final statement, "It's really about control, my body, my mind," turns into a series of confusing questions, "Who was going to own it? Them? Or me?" But these questions are merely rhetorical remarks that she and the film avoid answering. In confusion she confesses, "I'm not a one-man woman. Bottom line" (*Gotta,* 361). Nola's interpretation provides an uneasy closure to *She's Gotta Have It.* Her monologue and the film's conclusion reveal Lee's disturbing image of black feminist subjectivity, since his representation of Nola's sexuality is not as transparently independent as his film would have us believe. Nola might not be a "one-man woman," but three men could easily own and determine her mind and body in Lee's narrative.

Just as colonial fantasies welcome all physical, psychological, and economic forms of victimization of a *racial* other, Nola is colonized in a discourse that arouses male fantasies of a masochistic and insatiable *sexual* (m)other who welcomes all rapes. The objectification of black women in popular narratives manifests the architect's appropriation of patriarchal formulas to amuse the largest audience. I have suggested that minstrelsy permits covert racism through the black actor's participation in a popular Euro-American comedic form. Correspondingly, *She's Gotta Have It* allows a surreptitious sexism through a female's presence in a black urban folk comedy about a sexually "liberated" black woman. Nola's portrait permits audiences to view an oversexed black woman who consents to rape. In addition, her closest lover carries out this rape as a "loving" form of punishment.

She's Gotta Have It exemplifies how an urban black comedy film can seduce its audiences. First, it purposely obscures its misogyny by using elements of black life that oblige its black audience to feel proud and receptive. Second, it disorients the audience that has little understanding of black experiences. Both audiences might celebrate black film by uncritically accepting its sociological rendition of black reality. *She's Gotta Have It* employs condensed versions of black idioms. Its musical score includes a contemporary jazz soundtrack. African-American literature, the quotation from Zora Neale Hurston's *Their Eyes Were Watching God* (1937), opens the film. The mural in Nola's loft visually refers to Malcolm X, Bob Marley, the liberation struggle in South Africa, and recent racial killings of black New Yorkers. The film's dialogue makes verbal allusions to Alvin Ailey and Jesse Jackson (*Gotta,* 291, 319, 327). All of these sociocultural experiences of the African-American people, the many intimate associations and allusions that are part of the group's social experience, produce an Afrocentric type of urban comedy film. The collage of black photographs of past and present black life, the creative use of montage sequences in which fifteen black men rap (words used to seduce a female) directly into the camera (*Gotta,* 285–287), and the ingeniously funny love scenes between Nola and Mars reveal Lee's particular talent for this comedy subtype. But my acknowledgement of Lee's talent does not obscure my criticism of the film's masculinist narrative, which links Nola's self-awareness to a chain of misogynist fantasies.

She's Gotta Have It portrays black female sexuality as rooted in the body of Nola and in the speech acts and gestures of black men. Lee's construction of Nola resembles a patriarchal design: the sexually and mentally dispossessed woman whose body is a conquered terrain where men game, hunt, and create territorial boundaries through dating, marriage, and paternity. Nola's relationship to Jamie, Mars, and Greer reflects such a patriarchal construct. Her dependence on them resembles the colonized racial object's relationship to the sociopsychic forces that construct those colonized. Nola is to Lee's imagination what Dora was to Freud's—objects designed by phallocentric narratives.

Since urban black comedy film avoids racially tendentious narratives, this subtype might portray gender, class, and sexual orientation in a derisive manner. Though Lee may not have intended to lampoon the female protagonist of *She's Gotta Have It,* the film's phallocentric perspective constructs Nola's female sexuality the way blackface minstrel films ridiculously portray African-American life. Lee suggests that a sexual act has transformative qualities but Nola's sexual acts depend on male approval and do not liberate Nola from her sexual anxiety. Similarly, black heroism is not a lived action since most of these heroes, if we accept them as such, die at the hands of white villains or a sanctioned system of (in)justice—lynchings and capital punishment. Unfortunately, Lee (and others like him) is unaware that sexism is as unjust as racism. Consequently, his visual narrative is determined by a misogynist and heterosexist montage of fifteen bogus men who offer their sex to Nola; later in the film Jamie, Mars, and Greer exchange control over Nola's prone body. Nola's Thanksgiving dinner illustrates how the three men control the discourse at her dinner table and, later, remain in her loft while Jamie shares her bed.

The film narrative fails to create an image of a sexually independent black female protagonist who is comfortable among women as well as with men who have no sexual desire for her. If Lee intended Nola to embody a sexually independent attitude, then his film fails. This failure reflects a badly written script and the filmmaker's propensity to objectify women for the sexual liberation of certain types of men. Most likely the film's failure results from the shortsightedness of any young filmmaker who spends more time manipulating black urban idioms than developing an equally novel statement.

School Daze

Lee's second feature-length film, *School Daze,* tackles the problem of color-consciousness within the black Greek system at a traditionally black southern college. Wannabees and Jigaboos describe two different black student groups at Mission College. The Wannabees (also known as Gamma Rays) are black women who are light complexioned and have straight hair by birth or by their design. Their male counterparts belong to the Gamma Phi Gamma fraternity of which "Julian (Big Brother Almighty) Eaves" is the leader. The Gammas promote an African-American sociocultural consciousness but refuse to include Africa in their political agenda (*Uplift,* 190, 281). The Jigaboos are black women who have Afro hairstyles, have brown to dark brown complexions, and sometimes wear African clothing. Their male counterparts are "Dap Dunlap" and his group "Da Fellas." These six men dislike fraternity rituals and the general philosophy of the Gamma Phi Gamma fraternity. Unlike Gamma Phi Gamma, these men espouse pan-African ideas and want Mission College to sell the stock they hold in companies that do business with South Africa.

Unfortunately, the film presents additional problems that are insufficiently developed, such as intraracial class strife, the apartheid divestment movement, and the abuse of women in fraternity pledging rituals. The superficial introduction of important themes weakens the film's overall portrait of black college life.

The Church's Fried Chicken scene is one example of an undeveloped theme that could have been musically rendered. In this scene Lee attempts to explore class conflict within the African-American community. Young black Mission College men eating at a local Church's Fried Chicken encounter a group of young, uneducated black men. Lee describes these men as "a group of local yokels. These six guys appear to be in their twenties. LEEDS, the smallest one, is the leader. They stare in the direction of [Dap Dunlap] and company. All six wear Jerri curls, some have those plastic caps on their heads" (*Uplift*, 272). The black lower-class men instigate a verbal duel with the Mission College men (*Uplift*, 273–277). The audience is invited to dislike these men because they "deserve" the hatred warranted by such aggressive behavior. Lee reveals his class bias by referring to the locals as "yokels." His ridiculous portrait of the six local yokels is a tendentious joke played on uneducated black men who are objectified for the amusement of an audience that attends college. The meeting lacks any appearance of black solidarity and the verbal quarrel almost turns into a physical battle. Interestingly, these same students organized a South African divestment campaign at Mission College, yet their pan-African consciousness does not manifest concern for unskilled and unemployed African-Americans. The students' brief encounter with black disadvantaged men is both ironic and telling. Many college students experience a similar class hostility when they encounter the inhabitants of inner-city neighborhoods that border universities. Lee's unfinished portrait of class strife within the black community is as damaging to the film as his neglect to exploit its musical potential.

Considering the black musical style that constructs *School Daze*, the Church's Fried Chicken scene requires a musical closure. The absence of such underlines the director's inability to develop important issues within the traditions of black musical theater. The dramatization of the friction between Wannabee and Jigaboo women takes place in the "Straight and Nappy" song and dance production (*Uplift*, 154–157, 220–

222). This production is an example of a scene in which music and dance are fully integrated. This form of music and dance performance is not a part of the Church's Fried Chicken scene though it is as central to black culture as black hairstyle choices. If Lee had chosen to dramatize this scene musically, the Jerri curl men could have portrayed Wannabees while Dap and company maintained their Jigaboo status. From a musical viewpoint, their argument would integrate social commentary with song and dance, similar to the "America" sequence in the film *West Side Story.* Instead of a male variation on the "Straight and Nappy" routine, however, Lee offers slices of black college life without any significant comment on blacks outside the gates of Mission College. Finally, the film's uncertain conclusions are revealed by the self-reflexive shout "Wake up" in the last scene. "Wake up" might also suggest a nocturnal emission that warns the next generation to better its educational skills before losing its creative seed on fallow ground.

Do the Right Thing

Lee's third feature film, *Do the Right Thing,* introduces racial and ethnic hatred through the characters who frequent Sal's Famous Pizzeria. The pizzeria is located on a city block in the Bedford-Stuyvesant neighborhood of Brooklyn, New York. *Do the Right Thing* dramatizes growing racial hostilities between Sal, his two sons Pino and Vito, the black delivery man Mookie, and other Bedford-Stuyvesant residents.

Sal tolerates blacks who respect his rules, but his tragic flaw lies in his inability to make compromises with Buggin' Out and Radio Raheem, who represent a new generation of black urban toughs. Buggin' Out and Radio Raheem demand that rules be changed to reflect the pizzeria's African-American patronage.

Pino is disturbed by Sal's stubborn determination to remain in Bed-Stuy. He despises his father's black clientele and would like to see him sell the restaurant, and move his business to *their* neighborhood—Bensonhurst. Pino says, "Pop, I think we should sell this place. Get outta here while we're still ahead . . . and alive. . . . Couldn't we sell this and open up a new one in our neighborhood?"[6] Later, Pino tells his father: "I'm sick of niggers. It's a bad neighborhood. I don't like being around them, they're animals" (*Do,* 197). And Pino adds: "I don't want to be here, [and] they don't want us here. We should stay in our own neighborhood, stay in Bensonhurst" (*Do,* 198). But Sal quickly dismisses such backwardness, "So what if this is a Black neighborhood, so what if we're a minority. I've never had no trouble with . . . [these] people. Don't want none either, so don't start none. This is America" (*Do,* 198).

From Do the Right Thing. *Private collection of the author.*

Pino celebrates an ethnic-racial apartheid system in which ethnic and racial groups remain in their proper neighborhoods. Pino fears most blacks and creates reasons to hate them. Yet he admires black entertainers like basketball player Magic Johnson, comedian Eddie Murphy, and singer-composer Prince (*Do,* 183–184). In questioning Pino's racist logic, Mookie says, it "sounds funny to me. As much as you say nigger-this and nigger-that, all your favorite people are 'niggers' " (*Do,* 184). But Pino quickly replies: "It's different. Magic, Eddie, and Prince are not niggers. I mean, are not Black. I mean they're Black, but not *really* Black. They're *more* than Black. It's different" (*Do,* 184–185). Pino's confusion reflects his inability to deal with black customers and the black neighborhood. His minority status and close proximity to blacks produce an unwarranted fear of what might happen, and his distance from Magic, Eddie, and Prince permits exceptions to his generalized fear of blacks.

Though Vito secretly disavows racism, Pino forces Vito into a complacent acceptance of racism. Vito's combined indifference to racism and subserviance to Pino is characteristic of those who join violent mobs.

They are people who do not support racist violence in theory, yet they acquiesce to it in practice. Sal, Pino, and Vito represent a range of working-class reactions to ethnic and racial diversity.

Mookie works for Sal, admonishes Vito for his passivity, and debates the logic of Pino's blatant racism. Mookie also arbitrates the verbal boxing-match between Sal and the black twosome Buggin' Out and Radio Raheem. Mookie must decide whether he will maintain his job with Sal, or join the ranks of Buggin' Out, the resident black militant. Buggin' Out threatens a boycott of the pizzeria if Sal does not place African-American personalities on his pizzeria's "Wall of Fame." The wall *exclusively* features Italian-Americans but Buggin' Out argues that since Sal's pizzeria has a predominantly black clientele, the "Wall of Fame" should showcase a few black role models.

In one of the final scenes, racial tension mounts as Buggin' Out demands the inclusion of black personalities. Radio Raheem enters the pizzeria with his ghetto blaster (a large radio) blaring Public Enemy's "Fight the Power." This is Sal's and Radio Raheem's second battle over the radio. Again, Sal warns him to turn the music off, but his warning goes unheeded. Without reflecting on the outcome, Sal angrily crashes his baseball bat across the radio. The music ceases and Radio Raheem's loss of audio power is a virtual castration—now he must pump up the muscle.

A rapid-fire montage of reaction-shots visually inflames the sense of racial tension. Radio Raheem drags Sal across the counter and to the floor of the pizzeria. Italian-American police officers arrive, pull Raheem off Sal, and place a fatal choke-hold on Radio Raheem, who is silenced in the process. From castration to lynching, the big, black Radio has broken down. Again, there is a series of brief reaction shots that culminates with a long-shot of Mookie. He reflects on all that has transpired. In a fluid crane-shot, he picks up a trash can and throws it through the window of Sal's Famous Pizzeria. The neighborhood youth, angered over Radio's death-murder, and provoked by Mookie's decisive action, set ablaze the restaurant. The scene demonstrates Lee's directorial talent and Ernest Dickerson's photographic skill, but it lacks any constructive critique of the socioeconomic processes that promote misunderstanding between ethnic and racial working-class groups. In pointing to the lack of political cogency in the film, bell hooks, a black feminist, finds a "distressingly nihilistic ritual of disempowerment is enacted when a large crowd of black people watch as a 'few' policemen brutally murder a young black man. Such a scene delivers a powerful message in a white supremacist society." hooks says the message reassures the policing forces that blacks are incapable of defending themselves and will be passive spectators to their own lynchings.[7]

The film elicited various judgments. Most of the debate centered on whether the film would ameliorate or worsen America's racial and ethnic tensions. In commenting on the film's reception by white audiences, hooks believes that "privileged elite white folks can be reassured that they are not 'racist' since they do not espouse the crude racism expressed by Sal and his sons. Yet the film (via these same white men) can also legitimate racist folks by providing a public space where suppressed racist slurs and verbal assaults can be voiced and heard."[8]

hooks states that the film may "legitimate racist folks," but it also permits nonracist modes of interpretation. One illustration of the chameleonlike quality of reception was documented when *Chicago Tribune* movie critic Gene Siskel interviewed Nick and Al, two Italian-American pizzeria owners who saw the film. Nick comments, "It really shows the way it is. It's funny. When I first got into the [restaurant] business, a guy told me 'Don't trust blacks.' " Al, Nick's brother, states, "I saw a lot of what we go through . . . in the picture." In commenting on the film's end, the brothers focus on the destruction of Sal's pizzeria, and overlook the death of Radio Raheem. Siskel, however, is quick to inform them of this oversight. Nick replies, "I'll be honest with you. I completely forgot about that kid dying. This Spike Lee is brilliant. He put so much violence in the destruction of the restaurant, that I didn't think about the kid." Al confesses his embarrassment and states that the cop handled it badly. Nick adds, "There were three cops on the kid. They didn't have to kill him. I think . . . one cop was venting his own anger. His own racism." The comments of the two pizzeria owners reveal the film's ability to evoke different reactions. Understandably, the brothers focus on the destruction of private property, a reflection of their immediate preoccupation as Italian-American pizzeria owners. Perhaps their shared Italian-American ethnic identity also explains Nick's and Al's identification with Sal. After Siskel points out the cruelty of the police, Nick recognizes the act of police brutality and its racist sources.[9] Nick's analysis demonstrates that ethnicity and race are not the sole determinants of the spectatorial gaze; there are also sociopsychic forces that color individual reception. Unlike the film audience, which is unaware of its subconscious motives for choosing to see a particular film, the producer, director, and studio consciously stress socioeconomic factors when they decide to make a film for a mass audience.

The purpose behind the production of Lee's *Do the Right Thing* recalls the production strategy that Melvin Van Pebbles articulated: "One of the problems we must face squarely is that to attract the mass we have to produce work that not only instructs but entertains." When critics remark that Lee's tilted angles, extreme close-ups, and fluid crane-shots create a style that separates Lee's films from standard movie fare, they should also note the socioeconomic and sociopsychic reasons for Lee's appropriation of an art school film style.[10] Lee's stylized camera technique in *Do the Right Thing* entertains the racially mixed film audience, the same group that made *She's Gotta Have It* a critical and financial success. His camera technique derives from the approach taken by Martin Scorsese (another New York University alumnus) in his first feature film, the independent production *Who's That Knocking at My Door* (1969). Just as the 1949 social problem films *Home of the Brave* and *Intruder in the Dust* had mixed purposes, *Do the Right Thing* dramatizes contemporary interracial conflict both to make a political comment and to enlarge box-office receipts.

Do the Right Thing imaginatively presents New York's burden of interracial animosity, which resulted in two infamous recent incidents between Italian- and African-Americans. One such incident occurred in December 1986 in the Howard Beach section of Queens, New York, where a group of Italian residents chased three African-Americans from a pizza parlor. The chase resulted in the death of a black who had fled into oncoming traffic. In reference to the Howard Beach incident, Lee writes, "I'm making an allusion to the Howard Beach incident by using a pizza parlor. The white kids in this case could be the sons of the owner of the pizzeria" (*Do,* 24–25).

On December 27, 1987, Lee's journal entry reads:

> While I was in the grocery today, I heard a radio newscast that two Black youths had been beaten up by a gang of white youths in Bensonhurst. The two Black kids were hospitalized. They were collecting bottles and cans when they got jumped. This happened on Christmas night. Just the other day some Black kids fired up a white cab driver in Harlem. New York City is tense with racial hatred. Can you imagine if these incidents had taken place in the summer, on the hottest day of the year? I'd be a fool not to work the subject of racism into 'Do the Right Thing' (*Do,* 32–33).

Lee goes on to discuss how his film will "introduce the subject lightly. People will expect another humorous film from Spike Lee." Later he confides, "The treatment of racism will have to be carried in the subtext till the end of the film. . . . Any approach I take must be done carefully and realistically. I won't make apologies. Truth and righteousness is on our side. Black folks are tired of being killed" (*Do,* 33). Lee's "truth and righteousness" rhetoric reveals that he believes his film will set the black story straight. But a radio newscast, as Lee noted earlier, had told of the growing tension between Italian- and African-Americans. Lee appropriated the coverage and rewrote it from a particular "black" point of view. "The look of the film should be bright. . . . I mean Puerto-Rican bright. AFROCENTRIC bright" (*Do,* 29). Although many Puerto Ricans and

African-Americans wear bright, colored clothing, some do not; has Lee denied them a place in his film? A later journal entry reads, "It will be told from a Black point of view. I've been blessed with the opportunity to express the views of Black people, who . . . don't have access to power and the media" (*Do,* 34).

Lee also reveals his partiality for black political nationalism. He writes, "The character I play in 'Do the Right Thing' is from the Malcolm X school of thought: 'An eye for an eye.' Fuck the turn-the-other-cheek shit" (*Do,* 34). Personally, I agree with Lee but neither my political agenda nor Lee's film can speak for all black people because such critical appraisals falsely attribute the many problems facing the black community to race alone. More than a decade before the appearance of Lee's films, film studios had appropriated black idioms to produce black action films—they, too, simulated an "AFROCENTRIC" realism. They, too, spoke in a singular black masculinist voice that silenced the others. hooks also finds Lee's stroking of his cinematic black muscle an all too sexist exercise:

> Many of the scenes highlighting the presence of black women in the film appear spliced into the central drama (various conflicts between men) like commercials. They take the heat off and replace it with erotic play. Every relationship between black females and males in this film has a sexualized dimension. Every black female in the film, whether she be mother, daughter, or sister, is constructed at some point as a sex object.[11]

hooks's comments underline why the struggle against racism must also be a struggle against sexism within and without the black community. The few black men who have leveled criticisms at Lee's myopic vision of black life in *Do the Right Thing* have yet to criticize Lee's portrait of black womanhood.

Stanley Crouch, an African-American writer, criticizes Lee's appropriation of black idioms to create a racist vision of American justice. He finds "it irresponsible when a successful, middle-class guy . . . makes a movie in which he essentially tells . . . the . . . black lower-class, 'Well, you're not going to get justice. They are out there to get you. It's you versus them. And this is what they do.' "[12] In a similar critical vein, black reporter Juan Williams criticizes Lee's use of black idioms that are peripheral to the core message of the film. "I believe Spike Lee gets lost here, in terms of all the sorts of radical chic aspects: of the pendants, the way they snap their fingers, the way they talk and the[ir] haircuts. When you get lost in all that, then you lose control of the larger vision. Then you get things like 'Tawana Brawley told the truth' scrawled on a wall. Nobody knows what it's about."[13]

Nearly two months after the June release of *Do the Right Thing,* another African-American died at the hands of Italian-American working-class youths. On August 23, 1989, four African-American youths entered the Bensonhurst section of Brooklyn and were met by a mob of forty Italian-Americans armed with baseball bats and a gun. The violence that followed left one black youth dead, fueled heated debates on New York's interracial strife, and increased popular interest in Lee's film. The media attention to interracial violence gave *Do the Right Thing* and Lee undeserved critical attention and unwarranted praise by well-meaning white liberals and certain members of the black community.

Lee appropriated the media blitz to promote his philosophy and to advertise the *blackness* of his film product. Consequently, Lee became a controversial figure and was elevated from a black filmmaker to urban sociologist. As mentioned earlier, Lee's use of black idioms seduces his audience into accepting a simulated form of blackness. His major black characters, Nola in *She's Gotta Have It* and Dap-Julian in *School Daze,* are as vaguely drawn as Buggin' Out and Radio Raheem in *Do the Right Thing.* Understandably, Lee's interracial audience celebrates his urban black comedies. His films are the most widely distributed filmic representations of urban black "reality," and Lee's ability to secure major studio distribution for his films encourages his popularity, the continuation of other studio-distributed black films, and the academic study of black film. Unfortunately, the distribution and consumption of his films also authorize his insular vision of black life.

As mentioned earlier, *Do the Right Thing* philosophically and visually resembles the black action films of the 1970s, a period in which black males swaggered on and off the screen while their women kept house and bed. Even Lee's use of contemporary urban music is a carryover from the 1970s musical scores of black composers such as Isaac Hayes (*Shaft*), Curtis Mayfield (*Super Fly*), and Melvin Van Peebles (*Sweet Sweetback's Baadasssss Song*) who wrote lyrics that enhanced the hero's street reputation. In *Do the Right Thing* rap music lyrically constructs and elevates the prestige of the tight-lipped hero Radio Raheem. The historical importance of *Do the Right Thing* lies in its revitalization of the black action film genre.

Like many mainstream film critics, Vincent Canby mistakenly places Lee in the vanguard of a new black cinema. He writes,

> It thus seems plausible that with Mr. Lee in the vanguard, we are about to witness the creation of a new black cinema, movies that speak with a singularly black voice. In addition to Mr. Lee's earlier films, we've already had Robert Townsend's satire, 'Hollywood Shuffle,' and 'I'm Gonna Git

You Sucka,' Keenen Ivory Wayans's sendup of the black macho movies exemplified by 'Shaft.'[14]

Contrary to Canby's findings, new black cinema includes African-Americans who work for major studios as well as those who work outside the studio system. Some examples of new black cinema are Warrington Hudlin's *Black at Yale* (1974) and *Street Corner Stories* (1977), Larry Clark's *Passing Through* (1977), Charles Burnett's *Killer of Sheep* (1977), and Alonzo Crawford's *Dirt, Ground, Earth and Land* (1978). All five of these feature-length films predate Lee's 1979 enrollment in the film school at New York University. Lee's film journals never recognize his debt to other black filmmakers, yet he borrows from their cinematic portrayals of urban black life and their use of contemporary black music. In fact, it is in Lee's imitation of these films that he continues the tradition of black filmmaking, and *assists* in the (re)new(al) of African-American cinema.

Canby's praise of Lee is misdirected and typifies the prevailing ignorance that characterizes mainstream critical discussions of African-American filmmakers. Such ignorance reflects the lack of scholarly publications on black studio-distributed and independent film. Unfortunately, the ongoing work of independent black filmmakers and video artists is ignored, and the variety of black voices is smothered by the masculinist and often homophobic black images that reign in major studio-produced black films.

Lee's film comedies represent just one form of the new black cinema, and his film style creates a false immediacy between the philosophy of black consciousness and its filmic depiction. Consequently, his audience accepts the simulations as socially realistic portraits of African-American life. Imitating Lee's urban black film style, major studios and their hungry black directors and writers borrow Lee's use of black speech, rap music, and funky dress. Many of these studio-produced black films further the process of simulation and create a sketchy form of black reality. In doing so, the films avoid dramatizing *other* equally important black problems such as sexism, homophobia, drug addiction, and AIDS.

In conclusion, *Do the Right Thing* constructs Sal's pizzeria and a Korean grocery as obstacles to the fruition of black community-controlled businesses. Such a focus permits the consumer, artist, and producer, intentionally or not, to avoid critical appraisal of a system that impedes black capitalism and discounts a community-based socialist alternative. There have been collective struggles to establish black-owned businesses. Efforts by the Black Muslims and Marcus Garvey are two examples of attempts to establish black-oriented enterprises. Sal's property rights, however, regardless of our dreams for a different economic system, are more important to the maintenance of capitalism than the wishes of Buggin' Out:

> Sal's Famous Pizzeria is private property. Sal is only in Bed-Stuy because he wants to run a business and to pass it on to his children. More than his whiteness, or his Italianness, that Wall of Fame represents Sal's rights as a property owner. In a sense, the whole American system is invested in that wall, and Buggin' Out is in no position to take on the system, nor is he smart enough to understand why.[15]

Lee is in no position to take on major studios, yet the apparent success of his militant rhetoric, which secured him the direction of the Malcolm X movie, would have us believe otherwise. Neither Lee nor Buggin' Out are the rightful heirs to the legacy of a Malcolm X or Martin Luther King since both men, in their separate ways, criticized the socioeconomic processes that disfranchise African-Americans as well as other *equally* marginalized people. *Do the Right Thing* does little to chart a path toward the empowerment of the Nuyorican and African-American folk it celebrates. Admittedly, Lee's film portrays an important social problem—inter-ethnic rivalry. But the film suggests that to celebrate black empowerment, African-Americans must deny an Italian-American small businessman his property rights. It is true that Mookie spared the life of Sal when he tossed the trash can through the pizzeria window, thereby diverting the mob from attacking a white man to attacking his property. The narrative elevates Mookie, through the death of Radio Raheem, to a leadership position but permits Mookie the liberal gesture of protecting his boss by destroying his property. Are property and boss separable, or are they two components of a single image that should be discarded? Even the Republicans, who cut federal funds for poverty programs, have supported black community-controlled capitalistic ventures. Like the bullied Vito who acquiesces to Pino's racist diatribes, Mookie is confined within a narrative that bullies him into a depoliticizing action. Property destruction does little to prevent either the fictional murder of Radio Raheem or the loss of real lives including the Chinese-American Vincent Chin and the African-American Yusef Hawkins, who were murdered by white working-class Americans threatened by the socioeconomic advances made by people of color.

6

Black Feminism and the Independent Film

This chapter focuses on films by black women and assists in the building of a black feminist theory of film production and reception by presenting a "womanist" interpretation of three aspects of black independent film. The chapter does not intend to prescribe conditions for black womanist filmmaking or its spectatorial readings. Nonetheless, the chapter considers how certain processes of representation and reception permit different readings of black womanist films. Finally, the words "African" or "black women" refer to the many black African women who survive and struggle in Africas throughout the world. Therefore, this chapter sets forth an international black womanist theory—a theory that rejects nation, race, gender, and class exclusivity—as derived from an analysis of black-directed independent films.

Throughout the chapter, the term "black womanist film" refers to narrative constructions as well as viewing positions that permit "womanish," as opposed to "girlish," processes of female subjectivity. Films belonging to this category dramatize the shared experiences of black women. I have borrowed the term "womanist" from the black author Alice Walker, who defines it as:

> A woman who loves other women, sexually and/or nonsexually. Appreciates and prefers women's culture, women's emotional flexibility . . . and women's strength. Sometimes loves individual men, sexually and/or nonsexually. Committed to survival and wholeness of entire people, male and female. Not a separatist, except periodically, for health. Traditionally universalist, as in "Mama, why are we brown, pink, and yellow, and our cousins are white, beige, and black?"[1]

From Cycles. *Courtesy of Women Make Movies.*

In relation to black film, the term womanist refers to black-oriented films (not their authors) and reading strategies whose narrative and receptive processes permit polyvalent female subjectivity.

The term "black womanist film" describes both the narrative content that constructs black womanist subjectivity and the various processes by which an audience might receive the narrative's construction of this

From Hairpiece. *Courtesy of Women Make Movies.*

subjectivity. The two levels articulate an ideology of black womanism as a twofold process of construction and reception. Black womanist film does not describe *all* films made by African and American diasporic women. However, black womanist film is the imaginative representation of the sociopsychic and socioeconomic experiences of African and African diasporic women. This film calls forth black womanist spectators and creates a spectatorial space for such an audience.

The concept of black womanist spectatorship should not be taken "to refer directly to the [black] woman who buys her ticket and enters the movie theater as the member of an audience, sharing a social identity but retaining a unique psychical history. Frequently, they do not even refer to the spectator as a social subject but, rather, as a psychical subject, as the effect of signifying structures."[2] Black womanist spectatorship, then, is a sociopsychic process, not a biological trait. It cannot totally exclude nor include its audience in terms of race or gender.

Black Womanism as a Form of Resistance

Black womanism is a form of resistance to a raceless feminism and to a phallocentric pan-Africanism. As a theoretical tool, it requires that one scrutinize how different audiences decode black womanist film. This is especially true for feminism and pan-Africanism, because each of these movements have ignored the triple oppression of black women. Black female subjectivity, as female and African, is historically positioned at the boundaries of gender, sexual orientation, and race. This subjectivity conjoins the two limit-texts of feminism and pan-Africanism, but heretofore has been on the margins of these discourses. Black womanist films resist dramatizing one-dimensional struggles that ignore the black woman's three-pronged oppression. For example, Safi Faye's *La Passante* (*The Passerby,* Senegal, 1972) criticizes the sexist expectations of a white French man as well as those of a black African man; Sara Gomez's *De Cierta Manera* (*One Way or Another,* Cuba, 1974 and 1977) presents sexism in post-revolutionary Cuba; and Michelle Parkerson's *Storme: The Lady of the Jewel Box* (United States, 1987) constructs black gay history while documenting the life of Storme, a male impersonator. These black womanist films question patriarchal and heterosexist notions of black female subjectivity. Each film also creates a viewing position that speaks to micro- as well as macro-struggles against *phallic* forms of knowledge and power within and without the black community.[3]

A womanist theory and practice of black films describes *possible* receptive processes. A womanist reception occurs only after an "interested" spectator actively participates in a systematic critique of the limitations of canonical (con)texts. Stressing the importance of an "interested" reader in the production of a plural text, Catherine Belsey writes,

> In the writable . . . wholly plural text all statements are of indeterminate origin, no single discourse is privileged, and no consistent and coherent plot constrains the free play of the discourses. The totally writable, plural text does not exist. At the opposite extreme, the readable text is barely plural. The readable text is merchandise to be consumed, while the plural text requires the production of meanings through the identification of its polyphony.[4]

Therefore black womanism, as a theory of reception and production, requires an "interested" spectator to decode the plurality of (con)texts, which include intra- as well as interracial forces that dehumanize the community. Black womanist critical strategies also interrupt the narrative continuity of systems and viewing positions that reduce racial, sexual, and class differences to one of gender. Black womanism, as Walker suggests, represents universalist notions of blackness that unite African and African diasporic cultures. Consequently, the black womanist film project constructs a *postNegritude* theory of reception and production.

Before defining the concept "postNegritude," I suggest the polyphonic quality of the movement and concept that preceded it and shares in its global concerns. Nigerian philosopher Abiola Irele writes that Negritude

> has acquired, in the way it has been used by different writers, a multiplic-
> ity of meanings covering so wide a range that it is often difficult to form a
> precise idea of its particular reference at any one time or in any one usage.
> The difficulty stems from the fact that, as a movement and as a concept,
> Negritude found its origin and received a development in a historical and
> sociological context whose implications for those whom it affected were
> indeed wide-ranging, and which ultimately provoked in them a multitude
> of responses [readings] that were often contradictory, though always sig-
> nificant. . . . The term has thus been used in a broad and general sense to
> denote the black world in its historical being, in opposition to the West,
> and in this way resumes the total consciousness of belonging to the black
> race, as well as an awareness of the objective historical and sociological
> implications of that fact.[5]

Similarly, "postNegritude" refers to any moment when members of the black community, through their literature, art, and politics, recognize that black culture "is, concretely, an open-ended, creative dialogue of sub-cultures, of insiders and outsiders, of diverse factions." Correspondingly, these members share a language of black subjectivity that celebrates "the interplay and struggle of regional dialects, professional jargons, generic commonplaces, the speech of different age groups, individuals, and so forth."[6] The recognition and shared productivity of the postNegritude project result from the active participation of an "interested" audience that decodes the black subject by using discourses that surround and construct representations of gender, race, class, sexuality, and nation. An "interested" audience scrutinizes the incorporation of these images (and how they reflect individuals and the community). Through this shared postNegritude recognition, black audiences will question their own (and, by implication, others') interpretations.[7]

Reception: Resistance, Accommodation, Assimilation

I propose three modes of black womanist film reception—assimilation, resistance, and accommodation (also referred to as appropriation). These three receptive modes represent the dialogic quality of any par-ticular black womanist film. In the resistance mode, a particular black womanist film may be rejected because it does not mirror a given audi-ence's partial vision of itself. The image that a group holds of itself may derive from an authorized hegemonic image, a resistant radical image, or a combination of the two which produces a tension for both viewer

From The Color Purple. *Courtesy of Pacific Film Archive.*

and the artist in question. This tension incorporates racial, sexual, and gender subjectivity. The blurring of racial, sexual, and gender hierarchies permits free zones of discourse and makes the black womanist project a most dynamic movement.

Since spectatorship is a physical phenomenon, certain black womanist texts permit viewing positions that criticize sexism but maintain black communal solidarity. Black womanist films that depict nonsexist men may threaten the psychologic desires of certain feminists—for example, separatists who deplore any feminism that includes men. In addition, nonblack feminist spectators who maintain allegiance to a raceless, classless, and heterosexist identity may deplore this form of black feminism, because it criticizes racial, class, and sexual discrimination within the women's movement. Nonetheless, such feminists may still enjoy black womanist films. Enjoyment demands that black womanist films represent, and their viewer-listeners identify with, some *nexus-of-desire* that results in accommodative readings of these films. The same criterion is also valid for raceless feminists and for pan-African spectators.

Certain pan-Africans might regard black womanist narratives as too hostile toward black patriarchal figures or might view black feminism as a threat to black communal solidarity because, according to them, the "natural" place for a black woman is within a nuclear family and one of her primary roles is to provide moral support to her husband. Generally speaking, this point of view naturalizes the subordination of women; it reflects a phallic hierarchical system rooted in false notions of black masculinity and femininity. Consequently, this phallic type of pan-African thought denies both male and female pan-Africans the ability to appreciate black womanist ideology as represented in film. Black psychologist Vickie M. Mays writes,

> The Afro-American woman has been denied power and privilege. She has been raised expecting to work, as she will need to assist in supporting her family. She will also be asked to do all she possibly can to advance the Black man and the Black race—at the cost of ignoring the oppression of sexism. Indeed, the Black woman has been taught from early childhood that one way to survive in this society is through marriage or in a male-female relationship.[8]

Pan-Africans who deny or devalue the oppression of black women demean black women as much as white feminists who disregard racial and class factors. When they view black womanist films, pan-Africans might both identify with the cinematic use of African and African diasporic elements and resist the elements that evoke identification with nonblack feminists. Thus, like some nonblack feminists, pan-Africans may assume an accommodative viewing relationship to a black womanist film.

Unlike the two accommodative positions discussed above, an assimilative reception tends to accept the film as a "realistic" vision, rather than a representation that revises the image of black womanhood. Assimilative spectatorial positions promote authoritarian conformity between creator, discursive apparatus, and consumer. Authoritarian discourses eliminate the tension between the desire to resist and the desire to accommodate. In the assimilative mode, audience members are at ease because their identity (their imagined subjectivity) is not threatened by seemingly contradictory images of themselves.

The process of authoritarian discourse is present in rigid systems as well as those contesting on the margins of discourse. Like any discursive apparatus, the black womanist film has an assimilative mode of construction and reception capable of denying "unauthorized" readings. If effective, this mode protects against uncritical acceptance and duplication of black womanist discursive strategies. Once black womanist theory moves from the periphery to the center, assimilative readings of black womanist discourses retain their protective strategies and oppose their initial pluralistic conception of black womanism. The move from liberation to repression occurs because modernist projects require a closure of their *imagined* boundaries—a reflection of the hegemonic culture's need to contain polyvalent subjectivity by maintaining segregated sites of "resistance," such as women's liberation, gay liberation, and black liberation. Black womanist subjectivity, however, blurs these imagined boundaries of black selfhood. This postNegritude blurring permits the dialogic possibilities of blackness in womanist film.

Since this book is an analysis of production and reception, I present here a brief overview of black womanist film production and borrow the words of black women to describe the polyvalent character of their films. Consistent with the American framing of this study, I direct most of my critical analysis to African-American womanist films. Yet it is important to understand that black womanist filmmaking is practiced in Europe, Latin America, and Australia.

Black Womanist Film Praxis

Some of the earliest work of black women filmmakers appeared in the 1970s and was filmed by black women from the Americas and Africa. Madeline Anderson, Sarah Maldoror, Safi Faye, and Sara Gomez represent the first wave of black womanist filmmakers. The beginning of an international black feminist film practice is seen in Anderson's *I Am Somebody* (United States, 1970), Maldoror's *Des Fusils Pour Banta* (*Guns for Banta,* Guinea-Bissau, 1971), Faye's *La Passante,* and Gomez's *De Cierta Manera*. Recent womanist films include documentary, experimental, fictional, and autobiographical works that focus on the lives and experiences of black women. Some United States examples of short films are Zeinabu Davis's *Cycles* (1989), an experimental film that deals with the experience of menstruation; Camille Billop's *Older Women and Love* (1987), which uses interviews to document love between older women and younger men; Ayoka Chenzira's *Hairpiece* (1982), an animated film that deals with black women's hairstyles; Julie Dash's *Illusions* (1982), a fictional film that features a black woman film executive during World War II; and Michelle Parkerson's *But Then, She's Betty Carter* (1980), which documents the life of a jazz vocalist.

African-British and black Pacific Islanders have produced womanist films that are as worthy of notice as their African-American counterparts. *Nice Colored Girls* (Australia, 1987) depicts a century of interracial intimacy between aboriginal women and white men and *Spread the Word* (1987), a video short by the same artist, deals with AIDS prevention. *Coffee Colored Children* (United Kingdom, 1988) portrays the experience of a girl who is of mixed racial parentage and who lives in a predominantly white neighborhood, and *Bastion Point* (New Zealand, 1980) documents the conflict over land rights between white New Zealanders and Maori indigenes. African womanist filmmakers, though few in number, have worked with both video and film. Goretti Mapalunga's *African Woman Broadcaster* (Zambia, 1989) presents the double-voiced pressures of the private and public spheres of black women media professionals. Wanjiru Kinyanji's *A Lover and Killer of Color* (Kenya, 1988) uses a poetic realist style to depict sexual exploitation and racial discrimination. All of these works have historical importance, but I will confine my analysis to two fiction films (*A Different Image* [United States, 1981] by Alile Sharon Larkin and *Losing Ground* [United States, 1982] by Kathleen Collins) and to the semidocumentary *The Passerby* by Faye.

In 1981, Alile Sharon Larkin explored sexism and African heritage in *A Different Image*. Interestingly, the film previewed at the Second International Women Filmmakers Symposium, which underlines the film's importance to a feminist audience. In addition to being a woman-centered film, *A Different Image* is forthright in its celebration of a pan-African consciousness that is at odds with Western sexism and racism. Larkin says,

The film deals with assimilation . . . of Western sexism and how racism is inherently a part of that, it really can't be separated from it. When I say that the racism and the sexism are inseparable, this also applies to definitions of manhood as well as womanhood.[9]

Larkin underscores the black womanist belief that racism is an inherent part of sexism, and to ignore this fact is counterproductive to the black womanist struggle for equality.

The film centers on Alana, a young black woman, and her friend Vincent, a young black man. After a male acquaintance ridicules Vincent's platonic relationship with Alana, Vincent tries to assert his manhood by forcing himself on Alana, who has fallen asleep on his bedroom floor. After Alana accuses him of attempting rape and severs their friendship, Vincent, missing her companionship, reexamines the question of the proper relationship between a man and a woman. Finally, he initiates a reconciliation by giving her earrings shaped like the Egyptian goddess Isis.

In the film, Larkin illustrates a touchy gender-related problem within the black community: black women are expected to submit to the sexual desires of their black male friends. Larkin does not limit this problem to the United States. By introducing the film with a collage of photographs of black women, and by using an African goddess as the symbol of Vincent's effort of reconciliation, Larkin underscores the correspondence between the experiences of black women throughout the world. She writes,

> If you look at Africa today, you see that people there face the same problem with sexism, [therefore,] I am saying that there were other cultures and other ways that men and women related to each other . . . before the African slave trade, before Islam, before the patriarchal religions came in. So, we have to study those ways before we [black people] took on these [patriarchal] values.[10]

Larkin understands the need for solidarity among black filmmakers around a commonly shared ideology that reflects a postNegritude openness to feminism. She writes, "An ideology or belief which attempts to compartmentalize the nature and form of the oppression of African people solely into gender and/or class, is ultimately destructive to our achieving genuine equality and liberation."[11] Larkin refuses to permit authoritarian ideologies of opposition to determine or speak for a black womanist film practice. She recognizes the ease with which some groups have co-opted the civil rights struggle to benefit their very white agendas:

> As a Black woman I experience all areas of oppression—economic, racial, and sexual. I cannot 'pick and choose' a single area of struggle. I believe it is in this way that feminists and other progressive whites pursue their own interests at the expense of those of us subjected to racism. They do not have to deal with the totality of oppression, and instead may conform to,

or accept the policies of, institutional racism. . . . Feminism succumbs to racism when it segregates Black women from Black men and dismisses our history.[12]

To understand *A Different Image* as an articulation of feminist ideas, as opposed to black womanist ideology, would be an aberrant reading and would produce the authoritarian mode of feminism. Larkin argues,

> The assumption that Black women and white women share . . . similar histories and experiences presents an important problem. . . . Both historically and currently, white women participate in and reap the benefits of white supremacy. Feminism must address these issues, otherwise its ahistorical approach towards Black women can and does maintain institutional racism.[13]

A pan-African reading that recognizes the abuses black women experience produces a different set of articulations and assumptions about the histories of women and men in the black community. For example, if the viewer focuses on the visual allusions to African women and on Alana's colorful dress, and if this viewer listens to the musical score, which connotes an African rhythm, then he or she might perceive Alana as the female representative of pan-African subjectivity, which, for the woman of color, is more dynamic than a generalized female subjectivity. I am not proposing that the black womanist and the feminist readings are binary opposites. I merely want to show that the same text can activate different accommodative readings for these two audiences.

A black womanist reading combines the latter two spectatorial positions—feminist and pan-African—and articulates the importance of the *refigured* African-American male, Vincent. This dialogic reading of *A Different Image* resists the processes of racial and gender closure. In discussing the problems of feminist thinking, Hortense J. Spillers writes, "Sexuality as a term of power belongs to the empowered. Feminist thinking often appropriates the term in its own will to discursive power in a sweeping, patriarchal, symbolic gesture that reduces the human universe of women to its own image."[14] Certain forms of black nationalism also belong to the empowered, and such nationalist thinking often appropriates the term "pan-African culture" in its own will to discursive power in a sweeping, patriarchal, symbolic gesture that reduces black humanity to its own image. Both of these reductive forms of empowerment deny the micropolitics of struggle within their specific groups. They attempt to force the assimilation of radical members by creating a politics of binary oppositions which discounts individual differences. Larkin's film dramatizes the micropolitics of difference within the black community and portrays the shared phallic notions that some men and women act upon. The film denies that a hypothetical sweeping, patriarchal gaze is biologically determined—the patriarchal gaze is an ideological construct that is figured in men as well as women. The film privileges the text constructed on pan-African historical subjects who are embedded in the *maternal* voice of Alana's mother and the embodied portraits of African women.

The black womanist reading-viewing position avoids the inherent sexual dualism that engenders both the "dominant male-centered position" and its appropriation by a "female-phallic" position. It acknowledges that the goal of black feminist theory is a revision of gender relations and an open-ended sexuality. Womanist goals do not attempt a simple appropriation of hierarchic systems that continue oppressive processes of subjectivity. Therefore, the black womanist film project proposes the collective revision of the pan-African community. Such a purpose requires the artist, critic, and audience to re-vision "possible" black others in a *postNegritude* world.

Larkin's *A Different Image* re-visions gender by denying that all black men are phallocrats and all black women are oppressed by such men. The film presents sexism as an ideological construct rather than a biological trait of the male. Larkin's film portrays how phallic ideas attract men, women, boys, and girls. According to the film, phallocentric thought is not limited to men; it is present in the baiting that Vincent receives from his male friend as well as the teasing that Alana receives from her female friend. Larkin's womanist film demystifies the totalizing effects of phallic ordering. The reconciliation of the Alana-Vincent friendship resists patriarchal closure. The idea that men are contentedly contained within a sexist system is revised, and the unquestioned fate of women as sex objects or reproductive apparatuses-in-waiting is denied. Larkin has presented a new image through her womanist vision of a male-female relationship. In Julie Dash's *Daughters of the Dust* (1991), womanism is again dramatized in a female-centered narrative with a pan-African sentiment. *Daughters* explores a family of Gullah women who celebrate their African heritage.[15]

The Womanist Film and the Black Professional

In 1982, Kathleen Collins directed *Losing Ground,* the first feature-length film made by an African-American woman. Like Larkin, Collins dramatized a critique of sexism in her film. She did not share, however, the pan-African sensibility of Larkin's film. The protagonist Sara is a black professor of philosophy who is married to an insensitive black artist. Distressed by her husband's interest in an attractive, extroverted Puerto Rican woman, the introverted Sara reevaluates her career, mar-

Kathleen Collins. *Photograph by the author.*

riage, and life. Altering her inhibited beliefs about the proper behavior of women professors, Sara takes a role as Frankie, a dramatization of the story in which Frankie shoots and kills her boy friend Johnny because he has proved unfaithful. At the end of the film, Sara, turning the blank pistol away from the man playing Johnny, symbolically points it at her own philandering husband. *Losing Ground* marks the first appearance of a black professional woman as protagonist in black independent films, and it is one of a very few portrayals of developing feminist consciousness in a black professional woman in any feature-length film.

It is beneficial neither to feminism nor black womanist creativity to collapse the socioeconomic differences of race and gender into a generalized feminist or women's film aesthetic of purity. Collins speaks of an "imperfect synthesis" of the African-American condition. She is "willing to recognize that being Black is without purity. That one cannot achieve [racial] purity in . . . [American] culture. That one can only achieve some kind of emotional truth. . . . That's what characterizes my work. . . . I am much more concerned with how people resolve their inner dilemma in the face of external reality."[16] But Collins is quick to affirm the cultural differences between black women filmmakers and their white colleagues, and she acknowledges that such differences inform the aesthetic choices of these filmmakers:

> I would think that there is a Black aesthetic among Black women filmmakers. Black women are not white women by any means; we have different histories, different approaches to life, and different attitudes. Historically, we come out of different traditions; sociologically, our pre-occupations are different. However, I have a lot of trouble with this question because I do not feel that there has been a long-enough tradition.[17]

A few black filmmakers in Africa have represented black Africa through womanist discourse strategies in which the experiences of women are central to the film narrative. This is true of the first black-directed African feature film, Ousmane Sembene's *La Noire de* (Senegal, 1968), as well as other African films directed by black men.[18]

Concurrent with the development of black African cinema in the late sixties, Faye, an African-born Senegalese, directed a womanist film. Faye's first film, *The Passerby,* spoke of the Parisian experiences of an African woman who is preyed upon by African and French men. Interestingly, Faye was both filmmaker and the filmed subject since she performed the role of the female who is the object of both men's gaze. Taking a different approach, Laura Mulvey argues in "Visual Pleasure and Narrative Cinema" that the male gaze is an inherent and incontestable property of narrative cinema. Faye does not agree with the closed status of the gaze but views the male gaze as a matter of who is behind, who is in front of, and who constitutes the audience that participates in this relationship. In *The Passerby,* a ten-minute semidocumentary, she disrupts the male gaze upon female body parts by giving the female object a transitive quality and thereby both reverses the source of the gaze and provides an "other" meaning. A series of shot-reverse shots and point-of-view shots interrupts the authority of the male point of view, as well as its discourse, and exposes the polyvalent quality of the male gaze. *The Passerby,* however, confines its resistance to a heterosexual system of gazing, since the film imitates the male gaze.

As early as 1972, Faye constructed a black womanist gaze to resist dominant viewing relationships. In fact, *The Passerby* is a forerunner of Trinh T. Minh-Ha's *Reassemblage* (1982), an experimental film that uses traditional ethnographic film techniques to critique the assumptions of that tradition and its colonialist and sexist gaze at the African female. *Reassemblage* disrupts the ethnographic discourse that empowers the ethnographer and colonizes the "primitive" object. Trinh's film employs voice-over narration to critique its visual imagery. The film can be viewed as a celebration of the sexism and ethnocentrism that it attempts to criticize. The same could be said of *The Passerby,* but such simplistic

Safi Faye. *Photograph by the author.*

conclusions ignore each film's parody of the male as a colonizer whose discourse constructs the female as native other. *Reassemblage* presents the sexist and colonialist gaze of European anthropology as well as the myth of an objective pursuit of knowledge. A voice-over questions the veracity of the documentary narrative form, and as the aural assault thickens, the film graphically fractures into disparate images of Africa. Just as a unified male gaze is nullified in *The Passerby, Reassemblage* destroys the authority of the ethnographer. Both of these films self-consciously construct a vision that refutes patriarchal myths.

Faye's *The Passerby* and Trinh's *Reassemblage* share the womanist purpose of Larkin's *A Different Image* since all three films construct a womanist gaze at the female body. Each one also criticizes forms of sexism that cross racial boundaries. Yet, Faye rejects identification as a woman filmmaker:

> I never say that I am a woman filmmaker. I think I am a human being like the others. I never put someone under me but I never accept to be placed in a submissive position. The only difference between me and a man are my familial responsibilities. When I think about my daughter Zeiba, I say O.K., I am a woman. But when I think of my job or a film project, I am like the other African men.[19]

Faye's response presents two important points. The product should not be confused with its author any more than authorial intent should describe the final product. Faye also refuses the title of woman filmmaker because, according to her, her films are not solely about women. She views her work in a larger frame—a sort of womanist struggle to counter dehumanizing relationships that oppress men and women.

According to Faye, the filmic representation of black African women should not be limited to roles as either a mother or a professional. Faye, for instance, acknowledges that African Serrer customs form her concept of womanhood—womanism. She feels a deep commitment to motherhood, but is equally committed to filmmaking:

> Since I am an African woman, I was educated in this way. I have remained close to the traditional role of mother, and this responsibility is not a burden to me. I try to keep my job near my eight-year-old daughter. Men do not have the responsibilities of caring for children, because they have wives to care after them. When I think about this I realize that I am a woman. But I cannot be a filmmaker without being a mother. As an African woman filmmaker, the two are very much a part of me.[20]

Faye's womanist understanding of filmmaking includes maternal obligations that cannot be separated from professional duties.

Granted, the history of black filmmaking presents a discontinuous pattern of false starts and long production gaps. The archaeology of the black women's participation is more than a twenty-year effort to pioneer creative processes for the reception and production of racialized, sexualized, and engendered black subjectivities.

In the area of black womanist filmmaking, the construction of an open-ended black sexuality has been dominated by women. The few exceptions, however, deserve mention. Marlon Riggs's *Tongues Untied* (1989), Isaac Julien's *Looking for Langston* (1989), and his codirected *Passion of Remembrance* (1986) deal with black gay subjectivity. Spike Lee's *She's Gotta Have It* (1986) attempts a womanist narrative style, but its hint of a womanist voice is hushed by the opinionated talking heads of the three men in the protagonist's life.

Cultural studies and visual research must freely consult the sacred (legitimized) discourses on blackness as well as those deemed profaned· in order to make visible the histories of the ignored members of the black community, and to permit a dialogue within this community and across its imagined boundaries of race, gender, sexuality, class, and nation. Ultimately, to ignore the dialogic aspects of blackness is to further the dehumanization of the black community.

Male-Directed New Black Independent Cinema

The production history and critical reception of *Which Way Is Up?*, *Giant Step, Raisin, Sweetback,* and *Do the Right Thing* describes the problems that befall studio-distributed black-oriented films. Though many white-oriented films encounter studio restrictions, black film projects normally receive extremely low production budgets, narrow race-specific marketing strategies, and limited access to first-run movie theaters.[1] Regardless of these artistic and financial limitations, many blacks will seize any opportunity to work for a major motion picture studio because studio films receive company sponsored distribution and marketing as well as a guaranteed production budget. Blacks involved with major film studios also receive automatic publicity, which increases their sense of self-importance. Finally, a financially and critically successful black filmmaker, such as Spike Lee or John Singleton, gains a discernible amount of control over future projects, crews, and production budgets. Nevertheless, there are some black filmmakers who resist the calls of fame and increased production budgets. These filmmakers rely on financial sources such as grants from governmental agencies and philanthropic organizations as well as distribution contracts with foreign television stations such as Germany's ZDF, France's Antenne 2, and Britain's Channel Four.[2]

Chapter seven returns to the first chapter's discussion of the cultural history and production process of black independent filmmaking, but focuses on more recent examples of male-directed films in which empowered images of black women and men dominate the screen. These independent films, unlike those made by the early black film companies of the 1920s and 1930s, dramatize the lived experiences of the black lower-classes. I now return to the mid-1970s, a period when the black action film was popular, to discuss how black filmmakers renewed the tradition of black independent film production.

For the most part, the first wave of *new* black independent filmmakers of the sixties and early seventies received its training as interns in television studios and as students in university film school programs. However, documentary filmmaker and producer William Greaves had to leave the United States to acquire his film production skills. "It was pretty clear to me back in 1952," he states, "when I was trying to break into the industry that there was a wall of racism and discrimination that I could not possibly penetrate."[3] Greaves left the United States and found work in Canada. Between 1952 and 1963, he worked as an assistant director, sound engineer, film editor, photographer, and scenarist. The National Film Board of Canada gave William Greaves a well-rounded education in film production. By 1963, he had worked on nearly eighty Canadian films, yet on his return to the United States, major television and film studios still refused to offer him film production work.[4] Fortunately, his film production experience supplied him with the necessary managerial skills and self-esteem to establish William Greaves Productions in 1964.[5] Four years later, he accepted a job in public television and helped other blacks to obtain film production jobs.

In 1968, National Education Television (NET) hired Greaves as executive producer of the black-oriented news program *Black Journal*. NET initiated this program in response to the social activism of both the civil rights movement and the sporadic urban uprisings. *Black Journal* was "the first black national news program on American television" produced and directed by African-Americans.[6] It featured social documentary films that focused on issues such as segregated housing, discriminatory hiring practices, and other problems that affect middle-class and lower-class blacks. NET programs were aired on national public television stations, hence, *Black Journal* was seen by a national audience. The program influenced major commercial networks to schedule other black-produced news magazine programs. Later in 1968, for example, WABC-TV hired Charles Hobson, a veteran of *Black Journal,* to produce the program *Like It Is.* Hobson then hired a black staff to work on the new show.[7]

The critical success of *Black Journal* is apparent in its 1969 nomination for an Emmy Award and its 1970 Emmy Award for "Outstanding Achievement in Magazine-Type Programming." This recognition gave NET enough confidence to continue both the program and its production internship for aspiring young black filmmakers and news reporters.

While producing *Black Journal,* Greaves won awards for individual documentaries that were segments of the series. These *Black Journal–* sponsored documentaries include *Still a Brother: Inside the Negro Middle-Class* (PBS, 1968), a semidocumentary that discusses the growing schism between blacks of different socioeconomic levels, and *In the Company of Men* (1969), which documents labor conflicts. In 1970, Greaves left NET to direct, write, and produce social documentaries for private companies, governmental agencies, and the Public Broadcasting System.

Greaves's commitment to the development of black filmmakers was apparent from the numerous opportunities he offered to black filmmakers that major film studios had refused to hire. Under the experienced guidance of Greaves, NET's *Black Journal* gave such blacks as Madeline Anderson, Stan Lathan, Tony Batten, and St. Clair Bourne some of their first professional opportunities.[8] Bourne directed *Black Dance* (1970), Batten directed *Focus: South Africa* (1969), Lathan directed *Black Athletes* (1969), and Anderson directed *Malcolm X* (1969). In 1970, Anderson, after leaving *Black Journal,* produced, directed, and edited *I Am Somebody,* a documentary about four hundred female hospital workers who struggle with racial and economic oppression. In 1971, NET's Children's Television Workshop hired Anderson to produce, direct, and edit such programs as *Sesame Street* and *Electric Company.* Bourne, formerly an associate producer at *Black Journal,* gained additional recognition outside the show and produced over thirty productions. His *Let the Church Say Amen* (1971), a powerful documentary on the black church, has already become a classic in film courses across the country.

Because of NET's sponsorship, *Black Journal*'s critical acclaim, and the enlightened guidance of Greaves, black documentary filmmakers and their films became an important part of the American documentary tradition. Needless to say, however, these opportunities would never have materialized without pressure and inspiration from black political activists in the form of urban uprisings and organized civil rights lobbying.[9] Finally, since governmental agencies wanted to ameliorate the socioeconomic causes of urban uprisings and educate the American public, they preferred to finance and distribute social documentaries rather than experimental and fiction films.

During the late seventies, university film production programs offered black students opportunities to gain experience in fiction and experimental film production, and many black independent filmmakers received technical training in white educational institutions. Los Angeles, as might be expected, seemed to attract the largest group of black filmmakers who, because of personal choice or studio-imposed conditions, remained outside the production doors of the neighboring film studios. For example, Haile Gerima, Charles Burnett, Larry Clark, Ben Caldwell, Billy Woodberry, Alile Sharon Larkin, Julie Dash, Melvonna Ballenger, Carroll Blue, and Barbara McCullough are all MFA graduates from the University of California at Los Angeles and the University of Southern California. This generation of university-trained filmmakers, with the exception of Burnett, has remained independent of the major studios. Of this group, the first to produce black independent feature films were Gerima, an Ethiopian, and Burnett and Clark, African-Americans. Gerima's *Bush Mama* (1975), Burnett's *Killer of Sheep* (1977), and Clark's *Passing Through* (1977) typify the new black independent feature-length films made by black filmmakers on the West Coast.

Although Gerima, born in Ethiopia, did not come to the United States until 1967, he does not consider himself different from black American filmmakers. He says, "Even if I were to return to Africa, I would always protect my direct links with black America. It has given me the courage to discover myself. . . . At first, I considered myself Ethiopian rather than connected to black America. Black America helped to humanize me."[10] Gerima's *Bush Mama,* according to Bourne, epitomizes the nonlinear black independent narrative film from the West Coast.[11] *Bush Mama* tells the story of the awakening consciousness of Dorothy, a welfare mother whose husband is imprisoned for a crime he did not commit. Dorothy must raise her daughter in Watts, a Los Angeles inner-city neighborhood. On her return home, Dorothy discovers a white policeman attempting to rape her daughter. Like Sweetback's assault on two officers to protect Moo Moo, she protects her next generation and kills the rapist. Dorothy's violence is self-protective and leads to her psychological liberation.

Although *Bush Mama* typifies the black independent family film in several ways, it is also different from studio-distributed black action and black family films. Studio-distributed black action films portray interracial violence between black and white men. In contrast, Dorothy's violence protects her daughter from a sexual assault. Whereas black action films traditionally portray the empowerment of a black male hero such as Sweetback or Shaft, Dorothy's violence empowers the mother-daughter relationship. Dorothy's violent actions do not permit her to escape her socioeconomic conditions. In contrast, Sweetback's, Shaft's, and Superfly's violence is a vehicle of liberation. Dorothy must develop a consciousness that shields her family from further physical and sociopsychical destruction.[12] Violent spectacles are not the central focus of *Bush Mama*—violence here merely shows that Dorothy will no longer passively endure psychological and physical abuse directed at her and her family. Dorothy becomes an agent rather than an object.

Even though such black family films as *A Raisin in the Sun* (Columbia, 1961), *The Learning Tree* (Warner, 1969), *Sounder* (Twentieth Century–Fox, 1972), *Claudine* (Twentieth Century–Fox, 1974), and *The River Niger* (Columbia, 1976) portray injustices, they either avoid or make ludicrous the development of the hero(ine)'s political consciousness. Unlike some black family films produced by major studios, *Bush Mama* shows violence and sexuality as acts that protect and sustain the African-American family. Therefore, the film establishes Dorothy's maternal aspects without denying her sensuality. Gerima also avoids some of the stereotypes rife in American popular culture; Dorothy is neither a sexless mammy, an oversexed exotic primitive, nor a passively long-suffering black woman. Her husband is neither a sexless coon, an ebony saint, nor an oversexed and demanding tyrant.

Pre-1968 independent black-oriented films portray black hero(ine)s who nobly endure socioeconomic hardships and sociopsychic abuses. In contrast, *Bush Mama* suggests that protagonists who proudly endure dehumanizing situations are not to be idolized. Consequently, *Bush Mama* resists conventional closures that would reunite Dorothy's family or would permit her to escape her socioeconomic conditions. The film expresses the sentiment that permanent changes in the social system cannot take place within a fictional narrative. Yes, Dorothy retaliates against black-on-black crime, insensitive welfare workers, and police brutality, but the film suggests that these are personal changes and not socioeconomic or sociopsychic. Characteristic of his generation, Gerima believes that the practice of black independent filmmaking must be evident in the film's narrative form as well as its ideological content. Therefore, *Bush Mama*'s nonlinear narrative style, illustrated in the use of collages and abrupt editing, is a self-conscious formal technique to deter a classical Hollywood-like reception. Burnett, Clark, and Larkin also use this technique for similar political purposes. Avant-garde and experimental camera techniques also thwart the critical and spectatorial relationships that classical narratives usually enjoy.[13] I, however, recommend the use of a camera style that alternates between classical, avant-garde, and experimental techniques, such as Spike Lee's film style, which both guards against alienating many members of the black audience and ensures crossover appeal.

In 1973, Gerima began the production of *Bush Mama* and by 1975 he had received the finished print.[14] Since the demise of the Los Angeles–based Lincoln Motion Picture Company, this was the first time that a black California-based filmmaker independently produced, directed, edited, and distributed an independent feature film. In 1977, Burnett and Clark, also residents of Los Angeles, created and distributed their black independent films, respectively, *Killer of Sheep* and *Passing Through*.

Like Gerima, they used a nonlinear narrative style to describe the Los Angeles inner-city neighborhood of Watts.

Killer of Sheep also resembles *Bush Mama* in its pessimistic tone and its implication that no permanent changes have occurred or will occur in the socioeconomic status of the protagonists. Despite these similarities, there are important differences between *Bush Mama*'s portrayal of an unemployed mother and her awakening consciousness and *Killer of Sheep*'s portrayal of an employed father and his inability to achieve such an awakening. The major problems of Stan, the protagonist of *Killer of Sheep,* are different from those of Dorothy. Stan works in a slaughterhouse killing sheep. He remains faithful to his wife, despite an attempted seduction by a white woman, but he loses his ability to show her tenderness. Moreover, unlike the sensual Dorothy, Stan becomes so overwhelmed by his job and the social environment that he becomes bored with his wife.

Killer of Sheep also shows how sociopsychic circumstances create tension in a black lower-class family. When Stan's friends attempt to persuade him to join them in crime, Stan's wife chases them from the house. Stan responds to neither their request nor her action. Instead, he channels his frustrations into a critique of his son. Whereas Dorothy develops insight into the socioeconomic system, Stan never understands why the system has failed him. *Killer of Sheep* is quite different from most studio-distributed black family films because the film is devoid of the sort of optimistic ending seen in *A Raisin in the Sun*. Stan is a frustrated and impatient hero. His family does not escape their working-but-poor existence. A $10,000 check and a move to a better neighborhood never comes. Instead, Burnett shows that serious problems disrupt black family life even when black fathers are employed and are barely able to financially support their families.

Clark's action film *Passing Through* also depicts racially-based socioeconomic problems. Warmack, a jazz musician, wants to maintain the independence of his black jazz band. Believing that blacks must stay together as a community, Warmack refuses a contract offered by a white music company. To weaken Warmack's ensemble, the music company tries to implicate it in drug dealing and, later, authorizes the murder of a black friend of the band. Warmack avenges the death by killing the murderer; Warmack is then caught and imprisoned. After Warmack is released from prison, the band conspires to kill the head of the music company who had been controlling the drug trade in the black neighborhood. The violence in *Passing Through* typifies the action film genre. There are important ideological distinctions, however, which separate this film from those action films distributed by major studios. First, Warmack's approach to violence differs from that identified with *Sweetback* because Warmack's actions are premeditated and receive punishment—his jail sentence. Second, black action films like *Shaft* feature heroes who lack ties to the black community. *Passing Through,* however, shows how Warmack's political consciousness develops as a consequence of his ties to the black community of musicians. Adam, the hero of *A Man Called Adam,* never achieves Warmack's realization and dies a lonely and embittered man.

Generally, black independent filmmakers on the West Coast, such as Gerima, Burnett, and Clark, prefer to create characters who live in black inner-city communities and do not escape these communities. Both Clark and Gerima dramatize the developing self-assertion of the major protagonist, and Burnett presents characters who never achieve this empowerment. All three filmmakers, like those who followed them, create ordinary black characters whose sense of self is determined by sociopsychic and socioeconomic forces.

Because most of these black independent filmmakers are funded by art agencies, they can avoid the conventions that determine how a studio-distributed black film dramatizes social problems and controversial issues. For instance, meager production grants from both the National Endowment for the Arts and the American Film Institute do not permit the hiring of popular black stars who demand costly salaries. The form and narrative content of black independent films may be experimental, avant-garde, and highly political as long as they receive the approval of the boards that oversee the administration of film and video production grants. These production and stylistic freedoms permit black independent filmmakers to experiment with audio, visual, and performance methods that seem unrefined to audiences and film critics reared on Hollywood films. Thus, the use of non-star talent, innovative aural and visual narrative techniques, and abrupt editing (all of which are at odds with the classical Hollywood narrative style) make black independent films different in content and form from studio-distributed black films.

On the East Coast, the late seventies also witnessed a wave of new black independent fiction filmmakers. For the most part, these filmmakers acquired their technical skills in university film programs like those of their West Coast counterparts. For example, Warrington Hudlin earned an MFA degree from Yale, Marco Williams from Harvard, Ayoka Chenzira from New York University, Alonzo Crawford from Columbia, and Michelle Parkerson from Temple University. Two of these East Coast filmmakers, Hudlin and Crawford, have produced three independent feature films. Crawford's *Dirt, Ground, Earth and Land* (1978) imaginatively describes the effects of urban renewal on one black neighborhood. Like *Bush Mama* and *Passing Through,* this film dramatizes

the developing political consciousness of a black community that orga-
nizes against the real estate speculators. Hudlin's *Black at Yale* (1974)
and *Street Corner Stories* (1977) are documentaries and, therefore, are
beyond the scope of this study as are several other black documentary
films made by St. Clair Bourne and Parkerson.[15]

When I began this study in 1982, there were few examples of black independent filmmakers who also worked on studio productions. Now there is
a growing number of black independent filmmakers (such as Charles
Lane—*Sidewalk Stories,* Reginald Hudlin—*House Party,* Burnett—*To
Sleep with Anger,* and Lee—post-*She's Gotta Have It* films) who have
made and continue to make studio-distributed black films. These black
filmmakers and their films usually have a double-edged relationship with
studios. This relationship creates a sort of dual consciousness in which
filmmakers attempt or pretend to entertain the tastes of the broadest
audience (read static phallocentrism) while acting under the influence of
what Richard Wright calls "a folklore molded out of the rigorous and
inhuman conditions of life" and moving toward a re-visioning of Wright's
social notion of black folklore to include those marginalized because of
their gender and sexual orientation. Surely black folklore, like any other
folklore, has its phallocratic elements that resist the indeterminate nature
of reception. This indeterminate quality reminds one that studio-
distributed black films have to attract white and black audiences. Therefore, this mixed purpose permits (or requires) some studio-distributed
black films such as *A Raisin in the Sun* to be saturated with potentially
subversive readings.

Conventional film narratives refuse certain forms of racial and gender
empowerment that threaten the expectations of a conventional audience. Hence, studio executives and black filmmakers and writers must
find a happy medium between disparaging blacks and entertaining the
larger white audience. One need only recall the Columbia executives
who refused Hansberry's early screen drafts of *Raisin.* These films also
use conventional closures in which plots progress toward the reunion of
family, community, or nation. This formula demands a generic homoge-
nized morality in which malfeasance is punished. In contrast, black folklore empowers black artists to include the rigorous and inhuman conditions of black life. Studio-distributed black films may borrow from black
folklore elements and use inventive forms but they cannot deny conventional morality and its narrative rules. Thus, studio-distributed black-
oriented narratives and womanist story lines are diametrically opposed
because a black-oriented womanist practice confronts and disrupts the
existing racist and phallocentric hierarchies that construct conventional
morality and its narratives. Many, but not all, of the black university-
trained filmmakers in the 1960s and 1970s express a black womanist

ethic. A few of their younger black colleagues of the late 1970s and 1980s found studio distribution for their films that appropriated pan-Africanist and womanist ideas; *She's Gotta Have It* is but one example. This newer generation of black films exhibits double-talk that reverses the racial hierarchy, creates rupture and tension, and avoids any direct critique of the system of hierarchical construction such as was seen in *Bush Mama, Passing Through, Killer of Sheep,* and *A Different Image*. The satiric hybrid minstrel form exemplifies this racial reversal.

Next, there are the advertising, distribution, and exhibition demands that studios consider when attracting a crossover audience for black films. Burnett's *To Sleep with Anger* (Samuel Goldwyn, 1990) and Singleton's *Boyz N the Hood* (Columbia, 1991) received studio financing but were insufficiently advertised and had a limited distribution. Both films experienced distribution problems that resulted in the box-office failure of Burnett's *To Sleep* and canceled screenings of Singleton's *Boyz*. The failure of *To Sleep* and the success of *Boyz* exemplifies how certain black films resist, by their hybrid design, particular forms of commercial appropriation.

Burnett's film portrays a black middle-class family in which sibling rivalry and a demonic old friend threaten to destroy the family. The plot develops with occasional narrative interruptions that disorient the audience. The use of black southern folklore and superstition seasons the plot and differentiates the film from any previous studio-distributed black middle-class family film. Unfortunately, the film's failure at the box-office is evidence of the disturbing truth that black avant-garde techniques are not welcomed by and will not sustain the interest of the mainstream black moviegoer. This dilemma forces studios to refuse certain types of black films. Independent black filmmakers must rethink their options and decide whether the benefits of a studio are worth the corresponding artistic limitations.

Singleton's work is an instance of a film narrative that accidentally disrupts the distribution and consumption of a black action film. *Boyz* dramatizes the efforts of two black youths who want to attend college and thereby escape their violence-prone existence in south central Los Angeles. The black narrative is a conventional one that requires lower-class blacks to escape the community rather than ameliorate the conditions that spur such escapes into the mainstream. The screening of *Boyz* created outbreaks of violence in several cities. These outbursts from an audience of mostly black youths presented Columbia with the problem of guaranteeing the safety of the audience as well as the property of theater owners. Following the pattern of other controversial action films that evoked black eruptions of urban violence, such as Mario Van Peebles's *New Jack City* (New Line Cinema, 1991), the news coverage of the

From Boyz N the Hood. *Courtesy of the Museum of Modern Art Film Stills Archive.*

gang-related shootings increased the desire of inner-city youths to see *Boyz* while the reports of violence deterred both theaters and their middle-class audiences from participating in this cultural exchange. Consequently, some exhibitors will limit the screening of certain black films, and so, studios will allocate smaller budgets for future black-action films. Low production budgets confine black films to an "underdeveloped" look that black directors can neither control nor aesthetically defend. Each filmmaker must weigh the (dis)advantages and ask if this form of production ensures them and their films a respectable longevity. Film studios that market black products must establish *lasting* relationships with the black press, church, and advertising agencies as well as create new strategies to effectively market these films to nonblack audiences as well as an ever-changing black audience.

Because black independent feature-length filmmakers have a style that is different from that of studio-distributed films, film critics and historians must not evaluate independent films on the basis of their

From New Jack City. *Courtesy of the Museum of Modern Art Film Stills Archive.*

correspondence to, or deviation from, studio films. Instead, the critics and historians must analyze the independent film in terms of the film-maker's efforts to create films that explore serious social issues and present balanced images of black women, men, and the African-American community. In developing such a cultural, ideological, socio-economic analysis of black film, critics and historians must describe how, by what means, and to what extent black independent filmmakers have chosen to be responsive to the needs of the black community. For example, one should ask why certain black independent filmmakers use rough editing techniques in both the visual and audio narratives of their films and what purpose it serves. Another question one should ask is how black filmic images, which have been mainly created by white men either to denigrate or to entertain black audiences, are now used by blacks to educate their community. These questions can show how traditional film styles and conventional black stereotypes, which proliferate in studio-distributed films, now compete for the approval of an interracial audience.

In summation, chapters two through five discuss how ideological processes have determined the representation of race and gender in particular studio-distributed black films. Underlining the determinist nature of the narratives of studio-distributed black films, I also add that a film's uncertain reception permits subversive readings. I discuss the reception of *Sweetback* as an example of the uncertainty that reigns in the black audience. But I argue for politicized readings that disrupt the master discourses of racism and misogyny. I employ the terms minstrelsy, hybrid minstrelsy, and satiric hybrid minstrelsy to describe how race and gender are represented in comedy, family, action, and black comedy narratives. In their imitation of sexist and racist imagery, films such as *Cotton Comes to Harlem, Hallelujah,* and *Shaft* betray a colonial relationship to the dominant narratives on race and gender. When films such as *A Piece of the Action, Raisin,* and, to a lesser degree, *Sweetback* use popular generic forms but resist sexist and/or racist imagery, they reveal a postcolonial relationship between the black artist and the studio system.

In chapter five, I describe the satiric hybrid minstrelsy narrative form as a dualistic process in which an individual is racially or sexually objectified. Implicit in this description is a criticism of racial and sexual binarisms that promote essentialism. This book celebrates black filmmaking and the integration of black artists into the film industry. The celebration of blackness is a worldly affirmation and resists practices that create racial essentialism and homophobic and misogynist images. Edward Said writes,

> The whole effort to deconsecrate Eurocentrism cannot be interpreted, least of all by those who participate in the enterprise, as an effort to supplant Eurocentrism with, for instance, Afrocentric or Islamocentric approaches. . . . It was always a matter of opening and participating in a central strand of intellectual and cultural effort and of showing what had always been denied and derogated.

In this book I applaud the work of black filmmakers, their use of inventive camera techniques, and their blurring of film genres (the elements of a black postmodern rather than postNegritude practice). In the same breath, I acknowledge that these practices do not necessarily produce narratives that resist misogynist and racist forms of subjectivity. The work of black women filmmakers and a "womanist" ideological practice, however, will help future filmmakers resist a raceless feminism and a misogynist and overzealous pan-Africanism. We live in and against such master narratives. This study has shown when, how, and why certain black films imitate or resist dominant representations of race and gender. It also describes the agential processes by which black films and their audiences resist, appropriate, or assimilate racist and misogynist ideas that surround and, at times, consume them.

Notes

Notes to Introduction

1. Teresa de Lauretis, *Technologies of Gender: Essays on Theory, Film, and Fiction* (Bloomington: Indiana University Press, 1987), 6.
2. Ibid.
3. See Hazel V. Carby, "White Woman Listen! Black Feminism and the Boundaries of Sisterhood," in *The Empire Strikes Back: Race and Racism in 70s Britain,* Centre for Contemporary Cultural Studies, 1982 report (London: Hutchinson Education, 1988), 212–235; also " 'On the Threshold of Woman's Era': Lynching, Empire, and Sexuality in Black Feminist Theory," in *"Race," Writing, and Difference,* ed. Henry Louis Gates, Jr. (Chicago: University of Chicago Press, 1986), 301–316; Felly Nkweto Simmonds, "She's Gotta Have It: The Representation of Black Female Sexuality on Film," *Feminist Review* 29 (May 1988): 10–22; Pratibha Pramar, "Other Kinds of Dreams," *Feminist Review* 31 (Spring 1989): 55–65; and Jane Gaines, "White Privilege and Looking Relations: Race and Gender in Feminist Film Theory," *Cultural Critique* 4 (Fall 1986): 59–79.
4. De Lauretis, *Technologies,* 6.
5. Ibid.

Notes to Chapter One

1. See Henry T. Sampson, *Blacks in Black and White: A Source Book on Black Films* (Metuchen, N.J.: Scarecrow Press, Inc., 1977). Sampson writes, "Black participation in the business of motion picture production and distribution began in Chicago, Illinois, when in 1910 William Foster produced the first of a series of black-cast comedies," (1). Sampson also states, "William Foster is

credited as being the first black in the United States to produce films featuring black casts. The Foster Photoplay Company, with offices at 3003 S. Spring Street, Chicago, Illinois, produced several films between 1910 and 1916, including THE RAILROAD PORTER, a comedy . . . THE FALL GUY, THE BARBER, FOOL AND FIRE, MOTHER, and BROTHER," (68). See also Tony Brown, "Black Hollywood the Way It Was," *Tony Brown's Journal* (April–June 1983): 3, and Thomas Cripps, *Slow Fade to Black* (New York: Oxford University Press, 1977), 179. Cripps dates Foster's first film production at 1912 with the appearance of Foster's *The Railroad Porter.*

2. Cripps, *Slow Fade,* 79.

3. Lofton Mitchell, *Black Drama* (New York: Hawthorn Books, Inc., 1967), 47.

4. Illinois Writers Program, "The Negro in Illinois: Theater," unpublished manuscript, Vivian Harsh Collection, Carter G. Woodson Library, Chicago, 6–7: "The first productions presented by Negroes featuring Negro casts . . . were produced in the East around 1890; but Chicago did not see any of them for ten years. In 1900 the famous comedian Ernest Hogan . . . came here to star in the now historic play 'A Trip to Coontown' at the old Park Theater." This article, quoting from the *Inter Ocean* of 12 May 1901, also states that by " '1901 Chicago Negroes envisioned a theater' . . . for colored people exclusively, at which only colored talent will appear."

5. Daniel J. Leab, *From Sambo to Superspade* (Boston: Houghton Mifflin Company, 1976), 59.

6. Cripps, *Slow Fade,* 80.

7. Lindsay Patterson, ed., *Black Films and Film-Makers* (New York: Dodd, Mead & Company, 1975), 5.

8. "Negro Motion Pictures," *New York Age,* 31 July 1913.

9. In *Toms, Coons, Mulattoes, Mammies, and Bucks: An Interpretive History of Blacks in American Films* (New York: Viking Press, 1973), 8, Donald Bogle states that "the coon developed into the most blatantly degrading of all black stereotypes. The pure coons emerged as no-account niggers, those unreliable, crazy, lazy, subhuman creatures good for nothing more than eating watermelons, stealing chickens, shooting crap, or butchering the English language. A character named Rastus was such a figure."

10. Leab, *From Sambo,* 60.

11. Thomas Cripps, *Black Film as Genre* (Bloomington: Indiana University Press, 1979), 66. Cripps wrote that only a "tiny fragment" of *Realization* exists, "thus, we cannot study what may have been the earliest instance of a black success myth on film." The nonexistence of early black films by the Foster Photoplay Company, the Lincoln Motion Picture Company, and the Micheaux Book and Film Company's silent films, with the exception of *Body and Soul* (Micheaux, 1924), forces me to rely on black newspapers and the writings of film historians and critics.

12. Leab, *From Sambo,* 55.

13. Lewis Jacobs, *The Rise of the American Film: A Critical History* (New York: Teachers College Press, 1971), 91–92.

14. Leab, *From Sambo,* 13.

15. Pearl Bowser, *Oscar Micheaux,* Whitney Museum of American Art, The New American Film Series, no. 17 (New York, 22 May–10 June 1984). This pamphlet incorrectly states that *The Homesteader* opened in Chicago in 1918 when in fact the film did not have its premiere until 1919, according to the *Chicago Defender* 22 Feb. 1919, 11. See Sampson, *Blacks,* 44, where the author states that the novel *The Homesteader* is based on Micheaux's "experiences as a rancher and the characters in it were Negro substitutes for the white persons with whom he had been in contact." As seen in his successful dealings with white Sioux City Iowans, Micheaux's ability to give black-oriented themes a popular narrative form permits his work to attract an interracial audience.

16. Cripps, *Black Film,* 27.

17. See Sampson, *Blacks,* 45–47, for a discussion of the problems the film had with local censor boards in Chicago, Illinois, and Omaha, Nebraska. See page 98 for a synopsis of the film.

18. Leab, *From Sambo,* 79.

19. Cripps, *Slow Fade,* 189.

20. Based on the *New York Age*'s 25 Jan. 1920 coverage of the film's scheduled debut at New York's Lafayette Theatre on 27 Dec. 1920, I give 1920 as the film's date of distribution rather than the date Cripps cites in *Slow Fade,* 190.

21. Bernard L. Peterson, Jr., "The Films of Oscar Micheaux: America's First Fabulous Black Filmmaker," *The Crisis* 86 (1979): 138.

22. Leab, *From Sambo,* 76, 78.

23. This film was the first black-oriented talkie. The *California Eagle* reported that "An all colored cast is being assembled for the first of the talking pictures which Christie is to produce from the famous Octavus Roy Cohen stories. . . . Selected as the first story to be made into a talkie is 'The Melancholy Dame' " (16 Nov. 1928). In *Slow Fade,* Cripps writes that "The earliest of the black talkies, Christie Comedies . . . [began] as early as 1928, even before *Hallelujah!* [MGM, 1929] and *Hearts in Dixie* [Fox, 1929] were in the can," 222–223.

24. Harry Gant was formerly a Universal Pictures and Lincoln Motion Picture Company cameraman. For brief discussions of Gant's work as a cameraman, see Cripps, *Slow Fade,* 324, and Leab, *From Sambo,* 64.

25. See Phyllis Rauch Klotman, *Frame by Frame—A Black Filmography* (Bloomington: Indiana University Press, 1979), 65–66.

26. *California Eagle,* 23 May 1930. The article states, "Negroes are being supplanted in most every other occupation by whites and other races."

27. *California Eagle,* 12 Dec. 1930. In celebrating the merits of Hollywood the article announced, "Statisticians on Negro economics should not overlook the fact that $12,000 divided among the comparatively small group of colored citizens here means no little assistance towards alleviating the present crisis of unemployment and narrowed industrial conditions. This sum was paid to [black entertainers] . . . during the month of October."

28. *California Eagle,* 16 Jan. 1931. In quoting a *Variety* article by Mark Vance, the *Eagle* informed its black readership, "Colored show biz can only

shout in a few spots. In all the other spots it hasn't strength to shout, it can't even whisper. It's been hard hit. . . . Ethel Waters is the only colored star listed making records and last year the one and only Ethel made five records for Columbia."

29. Geraldyn Dismond, "The Negro Actor and the American Movies," *Close Up* 5 (Aug. 1929): 90–97. This article also appears in Patterson, *Black Films,* 117–121.

30. William Thomas Smith, "Hollywood Report," in Patterson, *Black Films,* 134–138.

31. On the eve of the Depression, Schiffman managed five of the seven theaters in Harlem. As the *New York Age* reported on 27 April 1929: "Closely following the announcement that the Lafayette Theatre management had purchased the Lincoln Theatre comes the information that this same company has taken over the Roosevelt, Douglass, and Odeon Theatres. . . . This puts five of the seven theatres catering to colored patronage in Harlem under one management.

"Leo Brecher is head of the operating company which controls these five . . . theatres and Frank Schiffman . . . is the general manager." Also see Sampson, *Blacks,* 50: "In February 1928, the Micheaux Film Corporation . . . filed a voluntary petition of bankruptcy. . . . In the latter part of 1929, the company reorganized with new capital and was incorporated as a new company. . . . At the time of reorganization, the officers were Oscar Micheaux, President; Frank Schiffman, Vice President; and Leo Bracheer [sic], Treasurer."

32. Sampson, *Blacks,* 50.

33. Cripps, *Black Film,* 40.

34. The Micheaux Book and Film Company and the Western Book and Supply Company are companies that Micheaux controlled, but The Micheaux Film Corporation (circa 1929) is not. These different names are used by both film critics and historians when they refer to films directed or written or produced by Oscar Micheaux. It is necessary to recognize that Micheaux did not control The Micheaux Film Corporation.

35. Even though Van Peebles exercised complete control over the production of his film, he still lacked the ability or desire to distribute his films independently as did Foster, the Lincoln Motion Picture Company, and (before the 1930 distribution of *Daughter of the Congo*) Micheaux.

Notes to Chapter Two

1. William J. Mahar, "Black English in Early Blackface Minstrelsy," *American Quarterly* 37, no. 2 (1985): 260.

2. Sigmund Freud, *Jokes and Their Relation to the Unconscious,* Vol. 8, *The Standard Edition of the Complete Psychological Works of Sigmund Freud,* trans. James Strachey (London: The Hogarth Press, Ltd., 1960), 100. Freud writes, "Generally speaking, a tendentious joke calls for three people: in addition to the one who makes the joke, there must be a second who is taken as the object of the hostile or sexual aggressiveness, and a third in whom the joke's aim of

producing pleasure is fulfilled. . . . it is not the person who makes the joke who laughs at it and who therefore enjoys its pleasurable effect, but the inactive listener." Freud describes an exchange in which the addresser merely desires to please an "inactive listener." Thus, the addresser may not find humor in the joke but capitalizes on the exchange value of the ridiculed object.

3. Arnold Shankman, "Black Pride and Protest: The Amos 'N' Andy Crusade," *Journal of Popular Culture* 12 (Fall, 1979): 237–238. He writes on August 19, 1929, that " 'Amos 'n' Andy' was first heard on network radio. The program quickly gained a national following. . . . By 1930 the program was more popular than any other show on the air, and its two stars were the highest paid performers on radio."

4. Thomas Cripps, *Slow Fade to Black: The Negro in American Film, 1900–1942* (New York: Oxford University Press, 1977), 269.

5. Joseph Boskin, *Sambo: The Rise and Demise of an American Jester* (New York: Oxford University Press, 1986), 173.

6. Shankman, "Black Pride," 244–246. Shankman cites W. P. Burrell of Newark, New Jersey, who wrote that the radio series "introduced . . . new and cleaner comedy." Burrell added, "Correll and Gosden were the first blackface entertainers not to use the word 'nigger' in their sketches." Shankman also states that of the 150 prominent black Chicagoans consulted about the proposed radio program, 90 percent reacted favorably.

7. M. M. Bakhtin, *The Dialogic Imagination,* trans. Caryl Emerson and Michael Holquist, ed. Michael Holquist (Austin: University of Texas Press, 1981), 424–425.

8. Cripps, *Slow Fade,* 269–270. Cripps writes, "Blacks had not minded—indeed, had enjoyed—Amos 'n' Andy on radio. But movies were different, for on radio one could fancy them in the mind's eye as genuinely black rather than as grease painted . . . whites. . . . Not only were the starring blacks buried in a white plot; their strong women, Ruby and Sapphire, were gone, along with the urban ghetto environment . . . and with them the opportunity for a black-centered dramatic conflict."

9. I would like to thank Ernest Callenbach for suggesting this.

10. Television situation comedies and variety shows such as *The Jack Benny Show, Amos 'n' Andy, The Flip Wilson Show, Sanford and Son, Good Times, The Jeffersons,* and *What's Happening* caricatured black men and women. The pervasiveness and longevity of these coon and mammy types tend to make viewers believe these images represent sociological facts.

11. Donald Bogle, *Toms, Coons, Mulattoes, Mammies, and Bucks* (New York: Viking Press, 1973), 8–9.

12. Nancy Levi Arnez and Clara B. Anthony, "Contemporary Negro Humor as Social Satire," *Phylon* 24 (Winter, 1968): 340.

13. Shankman, "Black Pride," 238–239. Shankman writes that "Benjamin Brawley, the distinguished black historian, denounced the program as one that degraded African-Americans. In Chicago, Bishop W. J. Walls, president of the Board of Religious Education of the A.M.E. Zion Church . . . insisted [the radio show] 'emphasized the moronic and silliest type of black man. . . . If a

woman is not a tool, . . . she becomes a senseless, bossy wife or a tyrannizing vampire, using no reason and aspiring to nothing worthwhile, even in a funny way.' " This article also discusses Robert Vann's crusade against the radio program. In addition to these critics of the radio program, the NAACP had lobbied against the airing of the *Amos 'n' Andy* television program "one week after the television premiere" (248).

14. Tino Balio, ed., *The American Film Industry* (Madison: University of Wisconsin Press, 1976), 315. Balio writes, "Television began its real commercial expansion in 1948. The number of sets in use soared by more than 1000 percent, from 14,000 in 1947 to 172,000 a year later. In 1949, the number went up to 1 million, and in 1954 to 32 million. By the end of the 1950s, nearly 90 percent of the homes in the United States had television sets. . . . Television had grown to replace the movies as the dominant leisure-time activity of the American people."

15. Freud, *Jokes,* 100.

16. In *My Life of Absurdity,* Vol. 2 of *The Autobiography of Chester Himes* (Garden City, N.Y.: Doubleday and Company, 1976), Himes writes, "On October 20, 1966, [Samuel] Goldwyn [Jr.] had bought an option for a year on six detective stories containing Grave Digger Jones and Coffin Ed . . . the said option to be renewed for one more year on October 20, 1967, or picked up by Goldwyn" (336). Thus, at this date *Cotton*'s producer was ready to produce a film adaptation of *Cotton* for which Goldwyn purchased the rights in October 1968 (360).

17. Bogle, *Toms,* 231. Bogle writes, "Ossie Davis's rowdy production *Cotton Comes to Harlem* opened the new decade. For years the black intelligentsia had sworn that if blacks were able to write, direct, and control their own films there would be more integrity on [the] screen. . . . But Davis failed to give his audience any insights into the black experience. His film with its idealized all-black world . . . took place in the ghetto and presented a crew of congenial coons, toms, and black whores. . . . It studiously played up not to black fantasies on a black world order but to white fantasies of a black world full of harmless stereotypes."

18. Himes, *My Life,* 340. Samuel Goldwyn had hoped that Himes would be able to write the screen adaptation: "I [Himes] said I didn't like the first treatment [that] Sam had had written by a television writer [Arnold Perl] who I thought was prejudiced. He [Sam] asked me if I would make a trial. . . . We agreed."

19. *Variety,* 1 January 1971, 11.

20. *Uptown* was written by Richard Wesley, an African-American playwright. First Artists, a company of which Poitier was a partner, produced the· film.

21. Arnez and Anthony, "Contemporary Negro Humor," 341. Also see Morris Michael Goldman, "The Sociology of Negro Humor," Diss. New School for Social Research, 1960, as quoted in William H. Martineau, "A Model of the Social Functions of Humor," in *The Psychology of Humor: Theoretical Perspectives and Empirical Issues,* ed. Jeffrey H. Goldstein and Paul E. McGhee (New York: Academic Press, 1972), 110. Martineau writes, "In an analysis of materials

dating back to the 19th century, Goldman (1960) declared 'that Negro humor in form and content is derivative of the Negroes' unique social position in American life (p. vi).' Goldman suggested that an explanation of Negro humor requires an understanding of the pattern of race relations at the time in which the humor occurred. This socio-cultural frame of reference is considered appropriate and vital."

22. Fredric Jameson, "Postmodernism and Consumer Society," in *The Anti-Aesthetic: Essays on Postmodern Culture,* ed. Hal Foster (Port Townsend, Wash.: Bay Press, 1983), 114. See also Freud, *Jokes,* 233. Freud discusses a humorous displacement that is comparable to the African-American blues riff "I'm laughing to keep from crying."

23. *Car Wash* was directed and scored by African-Americans Michael Schultz and Norman Whitfield, respectively. But the scenarist Joe Schumacher as well as the producers Art Linson and Gary Stromberg are whites.

24. Personal interview with Michael Schultz, 28 July 1987. In Barbara Zeutlin's and David Talbot's *Creative Differences: Profiles of Hollywood Dissidents* (Boston: South End Press, 1978), 202–203, the authors report that Schultz stated, "Audience reaction to the film was overwhelmingly positive. The picture, which had been produced for $2 million, made $10 million in the domestic market alone. Sales of the soundtrack album brought MCA a few million dollars more."

25. Jameson, "Postmodernism," 113–114.

26. Bakhtin, *Dialogic,* 424–425.

27. Martineau, "A Model," 110.

28. For example, *Sanford and Son* dramatizes the life of Fred Sanford, a lazy, gambling, junk man; *Good Times* features J.J., a coonlike teenager who is both loud and uncouth; and *The Jeffersons* portrays an upper-middle-class black couple who are constantly arguing and whose male member, George Jefferson, resembles George (Kingfish) Stevens, the scheming, professionally dressed con man of the "Amos 'n' Andy" show. Also see Gil Noble, *Black Is the Color of My TV Tube* (Secaucus, N.J.: Lyle Stuart Inc., 1982), 115. Noble writes, "As bad as the early days of radio were for black self-image, they were mild compared to what we are confronted with today. Television reaches far more people than early radio did, and when one views program fare, 'Amos 'n' Andy' lives on." Noble adds, "The program 'Sanford and Son' is the same denigrating format. Fred Sanford is the reincarnation of [Andy], displaying the same indolence and the same lack of respect for honest work and black women."

29. Jurij Lotman, *The Structure of the Artistic Text,* trans. Gail Lenhoff and Ronald Vroon (Ann Arbor: University of Michigan Press, 1977), 73, n. 9. My understanding of spectatorship recognizes that any given character is not static and his or her meaning to one spectator may not be shared by another spectator. Freud, however, later escapes some of this rigidity by acknowledging the technique of "unification." Still, Lotman's analysis is helpful for a more dynamic understanding of communication exchange.

30. Arnez and Anthony, "Contemporary Negro Humor," 340–342. The authors write, "At this time, the country seemed receptive to the social satire

which became the major element in much of [Dick] Gregory's humor. Notice that he began at a time when any public verbal confrontation about the sick relationship between whites and Negroes was little heard of." In addition, they acknowledge that African-Americans initially used "humor . . . as a psychological leverage for the sake of their sanity and as a weapon for survival against the harsh treatment from their oppressors. . . . as Negroes grew stronger and acquired some power, their humor was modified from the allegorical tales of Joel Chandler Harris about Brer Rabbit and the Fox [which I call hybrid minstrelsy] to the blasting satire of Gregory," which I refer to as satiric hybrid minstrelsy.

31. Freud, *Jokes,* 156–157. Also see his discussion of the technique of "unification" in *Jokes,* 35, 39–40, 66–69, 104.

32. Ibid., 105. Freud says "tendentious jokes are especially favored in order to make aggressiveness or criticism possible against persons in exalted positions who claim to exercise authority. The joke then represents a rebellion against that authority, a liberation from its pressures."

33. Ibid., 68.

34. Martineau, "A Model," 112. In discussing Joseph Boskin's article "Goodby, Mr. Bones," *New York Times Magazine* (1 May 1966), Martineau concludes, "Historian Joseph Boskin (1966) has written with insight about the social functions of Negro humor, particularly as reflective of changing times and the history of race relations. Tracing Negro humor from early folk to the contemporary, Boskin suggests that it consists of two elements: internal and external. [I refer to these as black comedy and hybrid minstrelsy, respectively.] The latter was predominantly a means of accommodation to white society, a means of survival. Boskin viewed internal or ingroup humor, however, as functioning to overcome the obstacles of discrimination." In addition, Martineau cites the Arnez and Anthony study "Contemporary Negro Humor" discussed above. He finds that their study's "primary thesis is that contemporary Negro humor . . . represents social satire. . . . As social satire, this humor, the bitter as well as the more mild, is interpreted as a means of criticizing and highlighting the incongruities in American society; it is viewed as a general agent of social change."

35. Zeutlin and Talbot, *Creative Differences,* 207–209.

36. Personal interview with Michael Schultz, 28 July 1987. Box-office draw refers to the potential of a star, director, and film to draw an audience into theaters. By 1976, Richard Pryor had entered into a deal with Universal studios. In *Richard Pryor Black and Blue* (New York: Bantam Books, 1984), Jeff Rovin writes, "Universal would pay Pryor nearly one million dollars a year for four years, for which they would receive the first right of refusal on six films Pryor might wish to make. . . . As part of the agreement, Universal committed itself to develop projects on its own for Pryor, buying novels or screenplays that they felt were suited to his talents. In any of these projects he chose to undertake, Pryor was guaranteed complete creative control" (128–129). Later that same year, Pryor signed a four-picture contract that stipulated, according to Rovin, "Warner would develop projects for Pryor and would have dibs on whatever Pryor films Universal decided not to make" (141). Schultz had made *Cooley High* (AIP, 1975) and *Car Wash* (Universal, 1976), two financially successful black commercial films, and Steve Krantz had produced *Fritz the Cat* (Cin-

emation, 1972) and *Cooley High,* both of which attracted the largest segment of the film audience—teenagers. Cecil Brown had written *The Life and Loves of Mr. Jiveass Nigger* (New York: Farrar, Straus & Giroux, 1969), and Carl Gottlieb was the co-scenarist for *Jaws* (Universal, 1975) and had been a writer for several Flip Wilson variety specials.

37. "In Dialogue with Michael Schultz," *Chamba Notes* (Winter, 1979): 7.

38. Louie Robinson, "Michael Schultz: A Rising Star Behind the Camera," *Ebony* (September 1978): 95.

39. Freud, *Jokes,* 85–86.

40. Lotman, *Structure,* 73. Lotman writes, "The initial elements of the text perceived by the addressee, besides having their own intrinsic meaning, are signals of certain codes or groups of codes . . . which already exist in the consciousness of the receiver. But as soon as the recipient of information is confirmed in his choice of decoding systems, he immediately begins to receive structural signs which clearly cannot be decoded in the chosen key. He may want to brush them aside as nonessential, but their repetition and obvious internal systemic arrangement do not allow him to do so. And so he constructs a second system which from that moment on is superimposed on the first."

41. Michael Foucault, *Discipline and Punish: The Birth of the Prison,* trans. Alan Sheridan (New York: Vintage Books, 1979), 26. Foucault rejects any notion of a natural order. He writes, "the study of this micro-physics [hegemony] presupposes that the power exercised on the body [and mind] is conceived not as a property, but as a strategy, that its effects of domination are attributed not to 'appropriation,' but to dispositions, manoeuvres, tactics, techniques, functions; that one should decipher in it a network of relations, constantly in tension, in activity, rather than a privilege that one might possess."

42. Ibid., 26.

43. Ibid., 26–27.

Notes to Chapter Three

1. Donald Bogle, *Toms, Coons, Mulattoes, Mammies, and Bucks* (New York: Viking Press, 1973), 27: "In the end the first all-Negro musical, *Hearts in Dixie* pinpointed the problem that was to haunt certain black actors for the next half century: the *blackface fixation.* Directed by whites in scripts authored by whites and then photographed, dressed up, and made up by whites, the Negro actor, like the slaves he portrayed, aimed (and still does aim) always to please the master figure." I concur with Bogle, but some black directors, black scenarists, and even black spectators have accepted blackface images for the promises of professional success, financial return, and the spectator's need for entertainment. The master narrative tends to determine most of what the film industry produces regardless of one's race and well-meaning intentions. Even so, reception is not so easily determined.

2. Andrew Dowdy, *The Films of the Fifties* (New York: William Morrow and Company, 1973), 90. Dowdy writes, "The decline of original scripts in favor of films based on popular novels [and plays] inextricably tied the larger studios to the increasing permissiveness of American fiction."

3. Genevieve Fabre, *Drumbeats, Masks, and Metaphor: Contemporary Afro-American Theatre* (Cambridge, Mass.: Harvard University Press, 1983), 13.

4. Henry Louis Gates, Jr., *Figures in Black: Words, Signs and the "Racial" Self* (New York: Oxford University Press, 1987), 49. Gates describes "Discourse of the Black" as "the literature that persons of African descent created as well as the nonblack literature that depicts black characters. The phrase, then, suggests both how blacks figured language and how blacks and their blackness were figured in Western languages. . . . I am speaking here of the black as both subject and object of literature."

5. Tino Balio, "Stars in Business: The Founding of United Artists," in *The American Film Industry,* 149: "United Artists was formed on February 5, 1919, as a distribution company to promote, exploit, and market motion pictures. . . . A key feature of the distribution contracts stipulated that each picture was to be sold and promoted individually. Block booking was out. In no way could one United Artists release be used to influence the sale of another UA picture."

6. Michael Conant, "The Impact of the Paramount Decrees," in *The American Film Industry,* ed. Tino Balio (Madison: University of Wisconsin Press, 1976), 359. Conant writes, "The antitrust prohibition on all block booking in 1946 gave three minor distributors equal access with the five majors to non-affiliated theaters. The decline in total picture output meant that even the affiliated theaters needed more first-grade films than the five majors could supply. These three minor distributors, a large part of whose films were relegated to the bottom half of a double feature program before 1946, found themselves able to bid for screen time in first-run theaters as equals to the five majors. United Artists . . . was able to induce many of the new independent producers to distribute through it after it secured open competitive access to the first-run screens of former affiliated theaters."

7. Garth Jowett, *Film: The Democratic Art* (Boston: Little, Brown and Company, 1976), 338: "After . . . 1946 when close to 1.7 billion dollars was paid by movie patrons to see their favorite entertainment, the fortunes of the American motion picture went steadily downhill, with only the odd year in which the decline has been momentarily halted. In the fourteen year period between 1946 and 1960, the average weekly attendance dropped from ninety million to forty million. More important, the expenditures declined even more sharply, from one fifth to less than one-tenth of the available recreational dollars." This is especially true of the 1956 and 1957 decline, which was the result of the release of pre-1948 Hollywood features to television. Also see Conant, "Impact," 361–362.

8. Barbara J. Molette, "Black Heroes and Afrocentric Values in Theatre," *Journal of Black Studies* 15, no. 4 (June 1985): 456: "A recurring phenomenon among Black people in the United States had generated a type of Black hero in theatre and art forms. This Black hero is an individual who has faced American racism . . . and sometimes without apparent overt provocation, gets tired of the racism. A decision is made and a stand is taken."

9. "True-To-Life Cussing May Deny The Seal for 'Take a Giant Step,'" *Variety,* 18 March 1959, 3.

10. " 'Take a Giant Step' Not Neglected By UA But by Public, Avers Exib,"

Variety, 27 April 1960, 15. Also see *Filmfacts* 3 (6 Jan. 1961): 331–312. These pages provide a synopsis of *Giant Step* and production notes and reviews from *Saturday Review* and *Variety.* Arthur Knight wrote in "SR Goes to the Movies: No Escape" (*Saturday Review,* 26 September 1959, 28), "No film to date—not even *The Defiant Ones* [UA, 1958]—has attempted to describe so explicitly what it means to be a Negro in a white man's world. . . . The Scotts are neither poor, nor ignorant, nor exploited, nor are they subjected to any virulent, Faubus-like white supremacy. They live in the north, where prejudice is of a su[b]tler, more corrosive kind."

11. Mel Gussow, *Darryl F. Zanuck: Don't Say Yes Until I Finish Talking* (New York: Da Capo Press, 1980), 191. See also Cobbett Steinberg, *Reel Facts: The Movie Book of Records* (New York: Vintage Books, 1982), 22.

12. Robert H. Welker, "New Image of American Black," *Variety,* 1 Feb. 1961, 7, 19.

13. Darwin T. Turner, "Dramas of Black Life from 1953–1970," *Iowa Review* 6, no. 2 (Spring 1975): 82–99. Also see Clyde Taylor, "Black Films in Search of a Home," *Freedomways* 23, no. 4 (1983): 226–233.

14. David Susskind to Sam Briskin, 13 March 1959. This and all other Susskind letters cited are in the David Susskind Papers, Wisconsin State Historical Society, Madison, Wisconsin.

15. Sam Briskin to David Susskind, 16 March 1959.

16. Sam Briskin to Paul Lazarus, 5 November 1959.

17. Harold Stern to Bernard Birnbaum, 1 June 1960. This letter is from Petrie's attorney to Columbia Pictures assistant treasurer-secretary Birnbaum. Also see Jack Pittman, "Real Things Vs. Studio Mockups," *Variety,* 20 July 1960, 23.

18. Arthur Kramer to David Susskind, 30 December 1959.

19. It should be noted that during the late 1950s and well into 1960 Africa was witnessing the Mau Mau liberation movement against British colonialists in Kenya, the Algerian liberation movement against its French colonialist government, and civil unrest in the Belgium Congo.

20. Gladstone L. Yearwood, "Toward a Theory of a Black Cinema Aesthetic," in *Black Cinema Aesthetics,* ed. Gladstone L. Yearwood (Athens, Ohio: Ohio University Center for Afro-American Studies, 1982), 71.

21. Robert K. Sharpe to David Susskind, 21 March 1961.

22. William Goldman to David Susskind, 3 April 1961.

23. "1961: Rentals and Potentials," *Variety,* 10 Jan. 1962, 58.

24. In "A Raisin in the Sun," *Ebony* (April 1961): 53, the author states, "with all obstacles overcome and the movie an accomplished fact, Columbia is eagerly awaiting the day when it can recoup its $1½ million investment."

25. James Baldwin, introduction to *To Be Young, Gifted and Black,* by Lorraine Hansberry (New York: New American Library, 1970), xii.

Notes to Chapter Four

1. In the chapter on independent film, I will discuss black filmmakers who rejected the American film industry and chose to work independently, deriving

much of their financial support from private corporations, nonprofit agencies, and federal grants.

2. *Time,* 8 August 1966 as cited in *Filmfacts* 9, no. 19 (1 Nov. 1966): 236.

3. *Variety,* 22 June 1966 as cited in *Filmfacts* 9, no. 19 (1 Nov. 1966): 236. *Variety* states, "according to production notes, the original screenplay was once planned by the late Nate (King) Cole."

4. Donald Bogle, *Toms, Coons, Mulattoes, Mammies, and Bucks: An Interpretive History of Blacks in American Films* (New York: Viking Press, 1973), 214. Explaining the studio's marketing strategy and acknowledging *A Man Called Adam*'s resemblance to seventies action films, Bogle notes, "The feature seemed to have a certain oppressive centered-in-the-ghetto air about it (perhaps because it was such an inexpensive film and because its producers shrewdly distributed it in ghetto areas), and certainly the idea of a jazz film itself appealed to black audiences. So, too, did the idea of a new black heel of an antihero. (This idea was later successfully picked up in 1971 with *Sweet Sweetback's Baadasssss Song* and *Shaft.*)"

5. Betsy Sharkey, "Knocking on Hollywood's Door," *American Film* 14, no. 9 (July/August 1989): 54. In her interview with the executive producer of *The Mighty Quinn,* a Caribbean detective story that features Denzel Washington and Robert Townsend, the film's executive producer Dale Pollock admits, "There aren't enough black marketing executives, and the studios just don't know how to market a black movie to a white audience. There is a sort of institutional racism. I don't know who to blame." Pollock intimates that it is not the individual but the institution that must change. Among the necessary changes are the integration of blacks into the studio marketing offices.

6. Arthur S. Link and William B. Catton, *An Era of Total War and Uncertain Peace 1938–1980,* Vol. 2 of *American Epoch: A History of the United States,* 5th ed. (New York: Alfred A. Knopf, 1980), 763. "The basis of King's philosophy was the doctrine of nonviolence or passive resistance. . . . Following King's example, black college students proceeded to challenge Jim Crow by deliberately breaking local segregation ordinances in peaceful and orderly fashion. Seeking to dramatize the injustice of such laws, the demonstrators offered no resistance to violence and actually courted arrest."

7. Godfrey Hodgson, *America in Our Time* (New York: Random House, 1978), 212. "The Mississippi experience raised the issue of non-violence, which had been latent in the civil rights movement from the start. Not that anyone advocated the use of violence as a way of achieving the movement's objectives: the question was whether a member of the movement had the right to use a gun in self-defense. . . . The issue surfaced as early as 1962. . . . By the summer of 1964, virtually every SNCC worker in the field was carrying a gun."

8. Ibid., 208. Hodgson writes, "In 1962 [Robert Parrish] Moses helped to set up the Council of Federated Organizations (COFO), an operating coalition among SNCC, CORE, SCLC and local NAACP branches to co-ordinate voter registration and other civil rights activities." He added, "In the fall of 1963, COFO organized a Freedom Ballot, to get blacks used to the idea of voting." Hodgson noted that the Mississippi Summer Project helped to register voters "in support of a Mississippi Freedom Democratic Party."

9. Ibid., 216–217. Also see Benjamin Muse, *The American Negro Revolution: From Nonviolence to Black Power, 1963–1967* (Bloomington: Indiana University Press, 1968), 150–151. This book tends to describe and analyze this period from a rank-and-file Democrat point of view. Sometimes Muse apologizes for the Democratic party's indifference to black political disfranchisement. This is apparent in his narration of the Mississippi Freedom Democratic Party episode at the Democratic National Convention.

10. Ibid., 222–223.

11. Reginald Major, *A Panther Is a Black Cat* (New York: William Morrow and Company, 1971), 66–70. Also see Link and Catton, *An Era of Total War*, 861–862. They write: "These new voices spoke in harsh and uncompromising tones. . . . There was Malcolm X . . . . utterances in behalf of black dignity, full equality at once, and no compromise with white men. There was Stokeley Carmichael . . . enunciating a doctrine of 'black power' that carried unmistakable overtones of violence. . . . Bobby Seale helped found the Black Panther Party for Self Defense in Oakland in 1966 to organize and instill self-respect among ghetto youths and induce better treatment from police by a series of aggressive confrontations and pressure tactics. . . . H. Rap Brown, an advocate of black power, urged guerrilla warfare against the white establishment."

12. Link and Catton, *An Era of Total War*, 863, and Hodgson, *America in Our Time*, 430–433. Both works discuss the National Advisory Commission on Civil Disorders March 1968 report. Hodgson's analysis of the Detroit uprising of July 1967 argues that police brutality was a logical reason for urban guerrilla warfare against the police.

13. Richard Wright, "Introduction: Blueprint for Negro Writing," in *The Black Aesthetic*, ed. Addison Gayle, Jr. (Garden City, N.Y.: Doubleday and Company, 1972), 317–318.

14. Larry Neal, "The Black Arts Movement," in Gayle, *The Black Aesthetic*, 273.

15. Ibid.

16. Etheridge Knight as cited by Neal in "The Black Arts Movement," 258.

17. I consider the black aesthetic primarily as a criterion of beauty. This criterion is not static; it changes according to differing black perceptions of beauty.

18. Etheridge Knight as cited by Neal in "The Black Arts Movement," 258–259.

19. Harold Cruse, *The Crisis of the Negro Intellectual* (New York: William Morrow and Company, 1967), 541, 542.

20. Melvin Van Peebles, *The Making of Sweet Sweetback's Baadasssss Song* (New York: Lancer Books, 1972), 13.

21. Ibid., 14.

22. Ibid., 15.

23. Ibid., 32.

24. Herbert J. Gans, *Popular Culture and High Culture: An Analysis and Evaluation of Taste* (New York: Basic Books, 1974), 14. Gans notes that taste culture is "for most people most of the time, a vicarious culture; it is not the lived culture which can be abstracted from the way people actually live, but a culture

which describes how the fictional characters of entertainment fare and the real characters of the news stories act. The relationship between the vicarious culture and the lived culture, or between art and life, is very complex; sometimes one imitates another, but most often they travel along separate paths. . . . most people treat it as something outside themselves, to be used for information, enjoyment, self-realization, therapy and escape."

25. "Big Rental Films of 1971," *Variety,* 6 January 1972, 9; also see "Cinemation Year Loss, $115,323. First New Quarter Up On *Sweetback,*" *Variety,* 28 July 1971, 3, which supports the belief that *Sweetback*'s box-office returns helped its distributor Cinemation come out of a sluggish economic period: "Jerry Gross' Cinemation Industries reported a loss of $115,323 (36 cents per share) for the year ended March 31, 1971, compared to a profit of $178,370 (56 cents per share) for the previous year. However, earnings for the first quarter, ended June 30, 1971, jumped to a record $184,861 (56 cents per share) compared to a loss of $17,127 (5 cents per share) for the same period last year, thus reflecting success of company's 'Sweet Sweetback's Baadasssss Song'."

26. Lerone Bennett, Jr., "The Emancipation Orgasm: Sweetback in Wonderland," *Ebony* 26 (September 1971): 106–118); Don L. Lee, "The Bittersweet of Sweetback/Or, Shake Yo Money Maker," *Black World* 21, no. 1 (November 1971): 43–48; and Abeke, "Van Peebles on the Inside," *Essence* 4 (June 1973): 36, 62, 75.

27. Huey P. Newton, *To Die for the People: The Writings of Huey P. Newton* (New York: Random House, 1972), 116.

28. Kuumba Workshop, *From a Black Perspective: A Searching and Critical Analysis of the Hit Film—Sweet Sweetback's Baaadasss Song* (Chicago: Kuumba Workshop, 1978).

29. Ibid., 5–6.

30. Ibid.

31. Ibid.

32. When one asks why Hollywood refused to create virile angry black heroes, the primary reason seems to be that it was not in their interests.

33. *Variety,* 15 July 1970, 3: "Cinemation Industries president Jerry Gross . . . flew to Hollywood . . . for a week of production meetings. The expansion of the new distribution and production company, which is the parent company of Chevron Pictures, Childhood Films and Cinecom Theatres, has increased its activity in financing new productions on a larger scale than before."

34. Van Peebles, *The Making of Sweet,* 15.

35. Here, I distinguish three forms of distribution networks: major studios such as Columbia Pictures, United Artists, and Metro–Goldwyn Mayer; major independent distributors such as Cinemation, American International Pictures, and Dimension Pictures; and black independent distributors such as Black Filmmakers Foundation, Chamba Educational Films, and Mypheduh Films. Black-American independent productions that are distributed by major studios or major independent distributors cannot be considered black independent films because they rely on the major studios' distribution outlets.

36. *Variety,* 6 January 1971, 11. It is true that two black-oriented comedies, *Cotton Comes To Harlem* (UA, June 1970) and *Watermelon Man* (Columbia,

July 1970), signaled Hollywood's interest in the black market. A *Variety* article entitled "Negro Themes, Stars & Race B.O." stated, "Paced by United Artists' *Cotton Comes To Harlem* with a rental figure of $5,200,000, there were several films in 1970 that clearly hit big with the Negro market in particular and with the general public as well. These included Continental's *Slaves*, Columbia's *Watermelon Man*, and Columbia's *Liberation of L. B. Jones*. The latter, not made with the Negro market in mind, turned out to be a prime favorite there."

37. "Roger Lewis Plans *Shaft* Sequel With Heavy Race Talent," *Variety*, 28 July 1971, 4.

38. Garth Jowett, "Towards a History of Popular Culture," *Journal of Popular Culture* 9, no. 2 (Fall 1975): 493–494.

39. I am not saying that any particular audience is more *correct* in their choice of entertainment than any other audience. In using these terms "politicized," "unpoliticized," and "uninterested," I intend to describe a particular black film audience (taste culture) at a particular moment (the viewing of a film). These terms are not meant to be prescriptive nor do they imply pathological behavior on the part of any individual filmgoer.

40. "Black-Owned Ad Agency on *Shaft* Credited for B.O. Boom, 80% Black," *Variety*, 28 July 1971, 5.

41. This mythology of black control in the making of black action films needs more critical scrutiny. In the demystification of black film production, I suggest criteria to distinguish black-oriented independent productions from major distributions such as *Sweetback* and black-oriented studio productions such as *Shaft*. Black audiences tended to assume that black directors, producers, and actors were able to control studio productions. Understandably, studios supported this myth, which helped them exploit black power dreams and benefit from the rentals of black action films.

42. Cited in James P. Murray, "Do We Really Have Time for a 'Shaft'?" in *Black Creation* 3, no. 2 (Winter 1972): 14.

43. *Variety*, 28 July 1971, 20. The *Shaft* sequels were not able to cross over into the popular film market because black-oriented fantasies were not to the taste of a white popular audience. According to UniWorld president Byron Lewis, many elements of *Shaft* had crossover appeal, including Parks (a *Life* photographer who was well-known in the white community) and Hayes (a singer who was popular in both black and white communities). A "crossover" black-oriented film is one that attracts both white and black filmgoers. This phenomenon has occurred with such films as Sidney Poitier vehicles, *Lady Sings the Blues* (Paramount, 1972), and *Sounder* (Twentieth Century–Fox, 1972). Also see *Variety*, 28 July 1971, 20. Understandably, *Shaft* did not attract many white moviegoers because the innermost desires of black action filmgoers demanded self-assertive black heroes; few white moviegoers would pay to see these types of films. The Black Power rhetoric of Shaft and the film's black environment was foreign to whites moviegoers who enjoyed James Bond films. Nonetheless, major studios churned out black action films for three successive years.

44. Hugh A. Robertson was the film editor for *Midnight Cowboy* (UA, 1969) and *Shaft* (MGM, 1971).

45. In commenting on having fired Joseph Sargent, the white director who

was initially hired for *Buck and the Preacher,* Poitier wrote: "after seeing the film, I suspected that the technical work I had done was not superior to Joe's work, and in some instances was clearly not as professional. . . . But I perceived that there were indeed differences in approach, differences fundamentally deeper than anything technical: important ethnic equalities were essential to give dimension to the characters of the screenplay. Harry [Belafonte] and I wanted black people and minorities in general to find in *Buck and the Preacher* a certain substance, a certain nourishment, a certain complement of self." Sidney Poitier, *This Life* (New York: Alfred A. Knopf, 1980), 330.

46. Daniel J. Leab, *From Sambo to Superspade: The Black Experience in Motion Pictures* (Boston: Houghton Mifflin Company, 1976), 262.

Notes to Chapter Five

1. Nancy Levi Arnez and Clara B. Anthony, "Contemporary Negro Humor as Social Satire," *Phylon* 24, no. 4 (Winter 1968): 340.

2. Ibid.

3. Mel Watkins, "Writing in Black and White," *Chamba Notes* (Summer 1980): 9.

4. Spike Lee, *Spike Lee's Gotta Have It: Inside Guerrilla Filmmaking* (New York: Simon and Schuster, 1987), 284. Subsequent references to this book are noted in the text by *Gotta* and page number.

5. Spike Lee, *Uplift the Race: The Construction of School Daze* (New York: Simon and Schuster, 1988), 113. Subsequent references to this book are noted in the text by *Uplift* and page number.

6. Spike Lee, *Do the Right Thing* (New York: Simon and Schuster, 1988), 196. Subsequent references to this book are noted in the text by *Do* and page number.

7. bell hooks, *Yearning: race, gender, and cultural politics* (Boston: South End Press, 1990), 176.

8. Ibid., 177.

9. Melvin Van Peebles, *The Making of Sweet Sweetback's Baadasssss Song* (New York: Lancer Books, 1972), 14. Also see Gene Siskel, "This Picture's as Good as 'The Godfather,' " *Chicago Tribune,* 25 June 1989, sec. 3, p. 22, cols. 1–4.

10. Gene Siskel, "Spike Lee's Mission," *Chicago Tribune,* 25 June 1989, sec. 13, p. 5, col. 2.

11. hooks, *Yearning,* 182.

12. "How Right Is 'Do the Right Thing,' " transcript of "Nightline," ABC News, 6 July 1989, 3. Future references to this transcript are noted in the text by *Nightline* and page number.

13. Ibid., 8.

14. Vincent Canby, "Spike Lee Raises the Movies' Black Voice," *The New York Times,* 28 May 1989, sec. 2, p. 14, col. 5.

15. Geoffrey Nowell-Smith, "Blackass Talk: Do the Right Thing," *Sight and Sound* 58, no. 4 (1989): 281.

Notes to Chapter Six

1. Alice Walker, *In Search of Our Mothers' Gardens* (New York: Harcourt Brace Jovanovich, 1983), xi.

2. Mary Ann Doane, *The Desire to Desire: The Woman's Film of the 1940s* (Bloomington: Indiana University Press, 1987), 8.

3. See Catherine Belsey, *Critical Practice* (New York: Methuen, 1980), 104–105.

4. Ibid., 105.

5. Abiola Irele, *The African Experience in Literature and Ideology* (London: Heinemann Educational Books, 1981), 67.

6. James Clifford, *The Predicament of Culture: Twentieth-Century Ethnography, Literature, and Art* (Cambridge, Mass.: Harvard University Press, 1988), 46.

7. Linda Hutcheon, *A Poetics of Postmodernism: History, Theory, Fiction* (New York: Routledge, 1988), 180.

8. Vickie M. Mays, "I Hear Voices But See No Faces," *Heresies* 3, no. 4 (1981): 75.

9. Alile Sharon Larkin, *"Your Children Come Back to You* and *A Different Image,"* lecture presented at the 8eme Festival Du Cinéma Des Minorités Nationales (Eighth Festival of National Minority Cinema) a Douarnenez, France, debate "Lutte Actuelle des Noirs Americains" (Debate on "The Afro-American Contemporary Struggle"), August 28, 1985.

10. Ibid.

11. Alile Sharon Larkin, "Black Women Film-makers Defining Ourselves: Feminism in Our Own Voice," in *Female Spectators: Looking at Film and Television,* ed. E. Deidre Pribram (New York: Verso, 1988), 158.

12. Ibid.

13. Ibid., 158–159.

14. Hortense J. Spillers, "Interstices: A Small Drama of Words," in *Pleasure and Danger,* ed. Carole S. Vance (New York: Routledge and Kegan Paul, 1984), 78.

15. Greg Tate, "Of Homegirl Goddesses and Geechee Women," *The Village Voice* (Voice Film Special), 4 June 1991, 72, 78. Unfortunately, a review copy of *Daughters* was not available when I wrote this essay.

16. David Nicholson, "A Commitment to Writing: A Conversation with Kathleen Collins Prettyman," *Black Film Review* 5, no. 1 (1988–1989): 12.

17. Loretta Campbell, "Reinventing Our Image: Eleven Black Women Filmmakers," *Heresies* 4, no. 4 (1983): 62.

18. Paulin Soumanou Vieyra, *Le Cinéma Africain: Des origines à 1973* (Paris: Editions Présence Africaine, 1975), 162.

19. Safi Faye, interview with author, Paris, France, 26 May 1986.

20. Ibid.

Notes to Chapter Seven

1. For an example of these studio practices see Michael Martinez, "NAACP Branch Drumming Up B.O. Business for 'Anger' Film," *The Hollywood Reporter* 314, no. 4 (October 1990): 3, 8.

2. Charles Burnett, interview with author, Chicago, 4 May 1984. Burnett stated that at the Berlin film festival showing of *Killer of Sheep,* he was approached by a representative of ZDF television who was interested in purchasing the German television rights to his next film *My Brother's Wedding* (1984).

3. James P. Murray, "William Greaves: Documentaries Are Not Dead," *Black Creation* 4, no. 1 (Fall 1972): 10.

4. Janine Euvrard, "William Greaves," in *Le Cinema Noir Americain,* ed. Mark Reid et al. (Paris: CinemAction/Cerf, 1988), 151–154.

5. Pearl Bowser, "Homage to William Greaves," in *Independent Black American Cinema,* ed. Pearl Bowser and Valerie Harris (New York: Theater Program of Third World Newsreel, 1981), 2.

6. For discussions of a black film aesthetic see Vattel T. Rose, "Afro-American Literature as a Cultural Resource for a Black Cinema Aesthetic," in *Black Cinema Aesthetics: Issues in Independent Black Filmmaking,* ed. Gladstone L. Yearwood (Athens, Ohio: Ohio University Center for Afro-American Studies, 1982), 27–40; Gladstone L. Yearwood, "Towards a Theory of a Black Aesthetic," in *Black Cinema Aesthetics,* 67–81; and Thomas Cripps, *Black Film as Genre* (Bloomington: Indiana University Press, 1979), 3–6. For a more production-oriented black film practice that views film style and film content as equally important to building a black independent cinema, see St. Clair Bourne, "The Development of the Contemporary Black Film Movement," and Haile Gerima, "On Independent Black Cinema," in Yearwood, *Black Cinema Aesthetics,* 93–105 and 106–113, respectively. Bourne writes, "Minority programming in the electronic mass media has had a relatively brief history. There have been sporadic appearances of minority oriented films or television programs on the commercial networks, but it was public television that took the first major, yet tentative, step in the wake of the urban disorders of the nineteen sixties with 'Black Journal'—the first black national news program on American television. The purpose was clear: to provide minorities with an opportunity to address each other on issues they considered important" (97).

7. Gil Noble, *Black Is the Color of My TV Tube* (Secaucus, N.J.: Lyle Stuart, 1981), 43.

8. According to Donald Bogle, "Images of Independence: African-American Filmmakers," in *Gallery of Greats 1991: Black Filmmakers,* edited by Donald Bogle (Milwaukee, Wis.: Miller Brewing Company, 1991), Madeline Anderson gained her first film production experience with documentary filmmaker Richard Leacock. In 1964, New York's WNET television, a PBS affiliate, hired Anderson to work on *Black Journal* from 1968 until 1969. In Michael Mattox, "St. Clair Bourne: Alternative Black Visions," *Black Creation* 4, no. 3 (Summer 1973): 32, Bourne states, "Bill Greaves is really to me, the Black Godfather of film in many ways. He was my first boss at N.E.T. He allowed me to do the things I never would have been able to do in my first year or second year. Also as executive producer of 'Black Journal' he helped start the N.E.T. Workshop from which . . . the majority of your black filmmakers and technicians are coming."

9. Bourne, "Development," 93–94. Bourne writes, "When I began to make films, the money and financial backing I received to produce these films was not

because of any kind of 'do-good I want-to-help-you' attitude. The power structure reacted to the political pressures which came from the black protest movement. . . . the whole poverty programs were created with black staff; access to the air was allowed; and in 1968, the Public Television Network created what was called 'Black Journal,' which was the first national one-hour monthly news investigation program."

10. Louis Marcorelles, "Haile Gerima: 'J'appartiens à la fois à l'Ethiopie et à l'Amérique noire,' " in *Le Monde* 7 July 1984, 11. Gerima says, "Même si je retourne en Afrique, je garderai toujours des liens étroits avec l'Amérique noire. Elle m'a donné le courage de me découvrir moi-même. . . . Au début je ne me sentais pas du tout appartenir à l'Amérique noire, j'étais éthiopien. . . . l'Amérique noire m'a aidé à m'humaniser."

11. Bourne, "Development," 104–105.

12. Steve Howard, "A Cinema of Transformation: The Films of Haile Gerima," *Cinéaste* 14, no. 1 (May 1985): 28–29, 39. Gerima says, "If I was interested in her violent act, the next logical scene would be prison. . . . But the stages of her assertion were more entertaining. In the first stage of her consciousness a young person snatches her purse. She is incapable of even defending her purse from a little kid. The second stage is the oppressive woman who represents the state [a clerk at the welfare agency] and commits silent violence against her; Dorothy retaliates in fantasy by breaking a bottle over the woman's head. The third level was when it affected her daughter.

"My obsessive theme deals with consciousness. . . . When do you begin to become aware of the fact that the world has to be changed, and what are the processes that lead towards that awareness? For Dorothy, when the oppressive tool came down on her daughter. . . . She stood her ground and asserted herself in very physical terms. . . . [I]t is with her consciousness that I ended the film and not at the logical conclusion of a conventional drama that would show that she went to jail," (29).

13. Yann Lardeau, "Haile Gerima: Pour un mouvement de libération culturelle," in *Le Monde Diplomatique* 364, July 1984, 5. Gerima says, "Traditional film narrative techniques require that filmmakers narrate their film in a similar style. Implicit in this requirement is the assumption that there exists only one narrative style. . . . Thus, we have a responsibility to reproduce this style. If black filmmakers perpetuate this Hollywood style for all the world . . . black film will be judged and evaluated according to the Anglo-Saxon cinematic tradition. It is not sufficient to merely reject these conventions, the struggle must be carried on within the film's narrative itself." ["Le cinéma conventionnel dit qu'on ne peut pas s'exprimer tel que nous avons l'habitude de le faire. Cette dictature implique qu'il y a seulement un langage cinématographique et un tempérament cinématographique. Nous avons donc une responsabilité linguistique. Si on perpétue cet Hollywood monolithique, cette règle d'un langage pour tout le monde, le cinéma ne représente aucun intérêt pour moi. Le cinéma Noir sera jugé et évalué selon le baromètre des Anglo-Saxons. Il ne s'agit pas seulement de ne pas accepter les conventions: la lutte doit porter sur le médium lui-même."]

14. Marcorelles, "Haile Gerima," 11. Gerima describes the production history of his two films *Bush Mama* (1975) and *Harvest 3000 Years* (1975): "J'ai tourné simultanément *Bush Mama* et *la Récolte de trois mille ans*. J'ai commencé *Bush Mama* en 1973, je l'ai achevé [en] mi-1974. Je suis alors parti en Ethiopie l'été de 1974. En dix jours, j'ai tourné *la Récolte*. Le montage m'a pris une année. En même temps j'achevais le montage de *Bush Mama*. Fin 1975, les deux films sortaient des laboratoires."

15. Because I have focused this study on feature-length fiction films (except for the shorter films created between 1913 and 1931 by the first black independent filmmakers), I am not including work of black independent filmmakers who made comedy or nonfiction films, most of which use a short format or a nonfiction style.

Selected Bibliography

Abeke. "Van Peebles On The Inside." *Essence* 4 (June 1973).

Altman, Rick. "A Semantic/Syntactic Approach to Film Genre." *Cinema Journal* 23 (Spring 1984): 6–17.

Arnez, Nancy Levi, and Clara B. Anthony. "Contemporary Negro Humor as Social Satire." *Phylon* 24, no. 4 (Winter 1968): 339–346.

Ashton, Charlotte Ruby. "The Changing Image of Blacks in American Film: 1944–1973." Diss., Princeton University, 1981.

Baker, Houston A., Jr. "Discovering America: Generational Shifts, Afro-American Literary Criticism, and the Study of Expressive Culture." In *Blues, Ideology, and Afro-American Literature: A Vernacular Theory.* Chicago: University of Chicago Press, 1984.

Balio, Tino, ed. *The American Film Industry.* Madison: University of Wisconsin Press, 1976.

Bass, Charlotta A. *Forty Years: Memoirs from the Pages of a Newspaper.* Los Angeles: Charlotta A. Bass, 1960.

Baudrillard, Jean. "The Ideological Genesis of Needs." In *For a Critique of the Political Economy of the Sign.* Trans. Charles Levin. St. Louis: Telos Press, 1981.

Beardwood, Roger. "The New Negro Mood." *Fortune* (January 1968).

Bennett, Lerone, Jr. "The Emancipation Orgasm: Sweetback in Wonderland." *Ebony* (September 1971): 106–118.

Birtha, Rachel Roxanne. "Pluralistic Perspectives on the Black-Directed, Black-Oriented Feature Film: A Study of Content, Intent, and Audience Response." Diss., University of Minnesota, 1977.

Bobo, Jacqueline. "*The Color Purple:* Black Women's Responses." *Jump Cut* 33 (1988): 43–51.

———. "The Subject is Money: Reconsidering the Black Film Audience as a

Theoretical Paradigm." *Black American Literature Forum* 25 (Summer 1991): 421–432.

Bogle, Donald. *Toms, Coons, Mulattoes, Mammies, and Bucks: An Interpretive History of Blacks in American Films.* New York: Viking Press, 1973.

———. "Uptown Saturday Night: A Look at Its Place in Black Film History." *Freedomways* 14 (1974): 320–330.

Bond, Jean Carey, ed. "Lorraine Hansberry: Art of Thunder, Vision of Light." Special issue of *Freedomways* 19 (1979).

Boskin, Joseph. "Good-by, Mr. Bones." *New York Times Magazine* (1 May 1966).

———. *Sambo: The Rise and Demise of an American Jester.* New York: Oxford University Press, 1986.

Bowser, Pearl. "Homage to William Greaves." In *Independent Black American Cinema.* Ed. Pearl Bowser and Valerie Harris. New York: Theater Program of Third World Newsreel, 1981.

Briskin, Sam. Letter to David Susskind. 16 March 1959. David Susskind Papers, Wisconsin State Historical Society, Madison, Wisconsin.

———. Letter to Paul Lazarus. 5 November 1959. David Susskind Papers, Wisconsin State Historical Society, Madison, Wisconsin.

Brooks, Tim, and Earle Marsh. *The Complete Directory to Prime Time Network TV Shows, 1946–Present.* 3d ed. New York: Ballantine Books, 1985.

Brown, Cecil. "Blues For Blacks." *Mother Jones* (Jan. 1981).

———. *Days Without Weather.* New York: Farrar, Straus & Giroux, 1983.

Brown, Les. *Les Brown's Encyclopedia of Television.* New York: New York Zoetrope, 1982.

Brown, Tony. "Black Hollywood the Way It Was." *Tony Brown's Journal* 2 (April–June 1983): 3.

Browne, Nick. "The Political Economy of the Television (Super) Text." *Quarterly Review of Film Studies* 19 (Summer 1984): 174–182.

Buchanan, Singer Alfred. "A Study of the Attitudes of the Writers of the Negro Press Toward the Depiction of the Negro in Plays and Films, 1930–1965." Diss., University of Michigan, 1968.

Burton, Julianne. "Marginal Cinemas and Mainstream Critical Theory." *Screen* 26 (May–August 1985): 2–21.

Buscombe, Edward. "Thinking It Differently: Television and the Film Industry." *Quarterly Review of Film Studies* 19 (Summer 1984): 196–203.

Colle, Royal D. "Negro Image in the Mass Media: A Case Study in Social Change." *Journalism Quarterly* 45 (Spring 1968): 55–60.

Conant, Michael. "The Impact of the Paramount Decrees." In *The American Film Industry.* Ed. Tino Balio. Madison: University of Wisconsin Press: 1976.

Cook, David A. *A History of Narrative Film.* New York: W. W. Norton and Company, 1981.

Cripps, Thomas. *Slow Fade to Black: The Negro in American Film, 1900–1942.* New York: Oxford University Press, 1977.

———. *Black Film as Genre.* Bloomington: Indiana University Press, 1979.

Cruse, Harold. *The Crisis of the Negro Intellectual.* New York: William Morrow and Company, 1967.

Crusz, Robert. "Black Cinemas, Film Theory and Dependent Knowledge." *Screen* 26 (May–August 1985): 152–156.

Davis, Angela Y. "Rape, Racism and the Myth of the Black Rapist." In *Women, Race and Class*. New York: Random House, 1983.

Diakite, Madubuko. *Film, Culture, and the Black Filmmaker: A Study of Functional Relationships and Parallel Developments*. New York: Arno Press, 1980.

Donahue, Suzanne Mary. *American Film Distribution: The Changing Marketplace*. Ann Arbor: UMI Research Press, 1987.

Dowdy, Andrew. *The Films of the Fifties: The American State of Mind*. New York: William Morrow and Company, 1973.

Dyer, Richard. "Paul Robeson: Crossing Over." In *Heavenly Bodies: Film Stars and Society*. New York: St. Martin's Press, 1986.

Ellis, John. *Visible Fictions*. Boston: Routledge and Kegan Paul, 1982.

Euvrard, Janine. "William Greaves." In *Le Cinema Noir Americain*. Ed. Mark Reid et al. Paris: CinemAction/Cerf, 1988.

Fabre, Genevieve. *Drumbeats, Masks, and Metaphor: Contemporary Afro-American Theatre*. Cambridge, Mass.: Harvard University Press, 1983.

Gabriel, Teshome. *Third Cinema in the Third World: The Aesthetics of Liberation*. Ann Arbor: UMI Research Press, 1982.

———. "Teaching Third World Cinema." *Screen* 24 (March–April 1983): 60–64.

———. "Colonialism and 'Law and Order' Criticism." *Screen* 27 (May–August 1985): 140–147.

Gans, Herbert J. *Popular Culture and High Culture: An Analysis and Evaluation of Taste*. New York: Basic Books, 1974.

Garrison, Lee C., Jr. *The Composition, Attendance Behavior and Needs of Motion Picture Audiences: A Review of the Literature*. UCLA Management in the Arts Program, no. 12. Los Angeles: University of California, 1971.

Goldman, Morris Michael. "The Sociology of Negro Humor." Diss., New School for Social Research, 1960.

Goldman, William. Letter to David Susskind. 3 April 1961. David Susskind Papers, Wisconsin State Historical Society, Madison, Wisconsin.

Goodwin, James. "Film Genre and Film Realism." *Quarterly Review of Film Studies* 8 (Fall 1982): 357–361.

Gunn, Bill. *Rhinestone Sharecropping*. New York: I. Reed Books, 1981.

Gunn, Giles. *The Culture of Criticism and the Criticism of Culture*. New York: Oxford University Press, 1987.

Gussow, Mel. *Darryl F. Zanuck: Don't Say Yes Until I Finish Talking*. New York: Da Capo Press, 1980.

Hairston, Loyle. "The Black Film 'Supernigger' as Folk Hero." *Freedomways* 14 (1974): 218–222.

Hall, Stuart. "Gramsci's Relevance for the Study of Race and Ethnicity." *Journal of Communication Inquiry* 10 (Summer 1986): 5–27.

Hansberry, Lorraine. *A Raisin in the Sun*. Playscript. n.p., n.d. David Susskind Papers, Wisconsin State Historical Society, Madison, Wisconsin.

———. *A Raisin in the Sun*. Scenario. n.p., n.d. David Susskind Papers, Wisconsin State Historical Society, Madison, Wisconsin.

Harcourt, Amanda, et al. *The Independent Producer: Film and Television.* Boston: Faber and Faber, 1986.

Himes, Chester. *The Autobiography of Chester Himes.* Vol. 2, *My Life of Absurdity.* Garden City, N.Y.: Doubleday and Company, 1976.

Hodgson, Godfrey. *America in Our Time.* New York: Random House, 1978.

hooks, bell. "Black Women Filmmakers Break the Silence." *Black Film Review* 2 (Summer 1986): 14–15.

———. "Counter-Hegemonic Art: do the right thing." In *Yearning: race, gender and cultural politics.* Boston: South End Press, 1990.

Howard, Steve. "A Cinema of Transformation: The Films of Haile Gerima." *Cineaste* 14, no. 1 (May 1985): 28–29, 39.

Hudson, Octavia. "Audience Racial Composition and Interaction as Determinants of the Appeal of Black Films to Whites." Diss., Harvard University, 1979.

Hyatt, Marshall, comp. *The Afro-American Cinematic Experience: An Annotated Bibliography and Filmography.* Wilmington, Del.: Scholarly Resources, 1983.

Illinois Writers Program. "The Negro in Illinois: Theater." Unpublished manuscript, Vivian Harsh Collection, Carter G. Woodson Library, Chicago.

"In Dialogue with Michael Schultz." *Chamba Notes* (Winter 1979): 6–7.

Jacobs, Lewis. *The Rise of the American Film: A Critical History.* New York: Teachers College Press, 1971.

Jerome, V. J. *The Negro in Hollywood Films.* New York: Masses and Mainstream, 1950.

Jordan, Jennifer. "Cultural Nationalism in the 1960s: Politics and Poetry." In *Race, Politics, and Culture: Critical Essays on the Radicalism of the 1960s.* Ed. Adolph Reed, Jr. New York: Greenwood Press, 1986.

Joseph, Gloria I., and Jill Lewis. *Common Differences: Conflicts in Black and White Feminist Perspectives.* Boston: South End Press, 1986.

Jowett, Garth. "Towards a History of Popular Culture." *Journal of Popular Culture* 9, no. 2 (1975): 493–494.

———. *Film: The Democratic Art.* Boston: Little, Brown and Company, 1976.

Jowett, Garth, and James M. Linton. *Movies as Mass Communication.* Beverly Hills, Calif.: Sage Publications, 1980.

Klotman, Phyllis Rauch. *Frame by Frame—A Black Filmography.* Bloomington: Indiana University Press, 1979.

Kotlarz, Irene. "The Birth of a Notion." *Screen* 24 (March–April 1983): 21–29.

Kramer, Arthur. Letter to David Susskind. 30 December 1959. David Susskind Papers, Wisconsin State Historical Society, Madison, Wisconsin.

Kuumba Workshop. *From a Black Perspective: A Searching and Critical Analysis of the Hit Film—Sweet Sweetback's Baadasssss Song.* Chicago: Kuumba Workshop, 1978.

Lardeau, Yann. "Cinema Des Racines, et Histoire Du Ghetto." *Cahier Du Cinema* 340 (October 1982): 48–52.

———. "Haile Gerima: Pour un mouvement de liberation culturelle." *Le Monde Diplomatique* 364 (July 1984): 5.

Lazarus, Paul N., III. *The Movie Producer: A Handbook for Producing and Picture-Making.* New York: Harper and Row, 1985.

Leab, Daniel J. *From Sambo to Superspade: The Black Experience in Motion Pictures.* Boston: Houghton Mifflin Company, 1976.

Lee, Don L. "The Bittersweet of Sweetback/Or, Shake Yo Money Maker." *Black World* 21, no. 1 (November 1971): 43–48.

Leonard, William Torbert. *Masquerade in Black: Blackface Biographies.* Metuchen, N.J.: Scarecrow Press, 1986.

Lesage, Julia. "Feminist Film Criticism: Theory and Practice." In *Sexual Stratagems: The World of Women in Film.* Ed. Patricia Erens. New York: Horizon Press, 1979.

Link, Arthur S., and William B. Catton. *American Epoch: A History of the United States.* 5th ed. Vol. 2, *An Era of Total War and Uncertain Peace 1938–1980.* New York: Alfred A. Knopf, 1980.

Lott, Tommy L. "A No-Theory Theory of Contemporary Black Cinema." *Black American Literature Forum* 25 (Summer 1991): 221–236.

Lubiano, Wahneema. "But Compared to What?: Reading Realism, Representation, and Essentialism in *School Daze, Do the Right Thing,* and the Spike Lee Discourse." *Black American Literature Forum* 25 (Summer 1991): 253–282.

Major, Reginald. *A Panther Is a Black Cat.* New York: William Morrow and Company, 1971.

Mapp, Edward. *Blacks in American Films: Today and Yesterday.* Metuchen, N.J.: Scarecrow Press, 1972.

Marcorelles, Louis. "Haile Gerima: 'J'appartiens à la fois à l'Ethiopie et à l'Amérique noire.' " *Le Monde,* 7 July 1984: 11.

Martineau, William H. "A Model of the Social Functions of Humor." In *The Psychology of Humor: Theoretical Perspectives and Empirical Issues.* Ed. Jeffrey H. Goldstein and Paul E. McGhee. New York: Academic Press, 1972.

Mattox, Michael. "St. Clair Bourne: Alternative Black Visions." *Black Creation* 4, no. 3 (Summer 1973): 32.

Maynard, Richard A., ed. *The Black Man on Film: Racial Stereotyping.* Rochelle Park, N.J.: Hayden Book Company, 1974.

Mitchell, Loften. *Black Drama: The Story of the American Negro in the Theatre.* New York: Hawthorn Books, 1967.

Molette, Barbara J. "Black Heroes and Afrocentric Values in Theatre." *Journal of Black Studies* 15 (June 1985): 447–462.

Murray, James P. "William Greaves: Documentaries Are Not Dead." *Black Creation* 4, no. 1 (Fall 1972): 10–11.

———. "Do We Really Have Time for a 'Shaft'?" *Black Creation* 3, no. 2 (Winter 1972): 14.

———. *To Find an Image: Black Films from Uncle Tom to Super Fly.* Indianapolis: Bobbs-Merrill Company, 1973.

Muse, Benjamin. *The American Negro Revolution: From Nonviolence to Black Power, 1963–1967.* Bloomington: Indiana University Press, 1968.

Muwakkil, Salim. "Art vs. Ideology: The Debate over Positive Images." *Black Film Review* 2 (Summer 1986): 26–27.

Neal, Larry. "The Black Arts Movement." In *The Black Aesthetic*. Ed. Addison Gayle, Jr. Garden City, N.Y.: Doubleday and Company, 1972.

Nelson, Richard Alan. *Florida and the American Motion Picture Industry, 1898–1980*. New York: Arno Press, 1983.

Nesteby, James R. *Black Images in American Films, 1896–1954: The Interplay between Civil Rights and Film Culture*. Washington, D.C.: University Press of America, 1982.

Nesterenko, Genevieve. "La Representation Du Noir Dans Le Cinema Americain Contemporain, 1960–1972." Diss., Universite De Paris, St. Denis, 1978.

Newton, Huey P. *To Die for the People: The Writings of Huey P. Newton*. New York: Random House, 1972.

Ngangura, Dieudonne Mweze. "Le Noir Dans Le Cinema American." Thesis, Institut des Arts de Diffusion-Brussels, 1976.

Noble, Gil. *Black Is the Color of My TV Tube*. Secaucus, N.J.: Lyle Stuart, 1981.

Noble, Peter. *The Negro in Film*. London: Skelton Robinson, 1948. Reprint. New York: Arno Press, 1970.

Null, Gary. *Black Hollywood: The Negro in Motion Pictures*. Secaucus, N.J.: Citadel Press, 1977.

Olusoga, Sikiru Ademola. "An Analysis of Black Motion Picture Patrons to Determine the Demand for Black Oriented Movies." Thesis, California State University, 1973.

Parish, James Robert. *Actors' Television Credits, 1950–1972*. Metuchen, N.J.: Scarecrow Press, 1973.

Patterson, Lindsay, ed. *Black Films and Film-makers: A Comprehensive Anthology from Stereotype to Superhero*. New York: Dodd, Mead and Company, 1975.

Peterson, Bernard L., Jr. "The Films of Oscar Micheaux: America's First Fabulous Black Filmmaker." *The Crisis* 86 (1979): 136–141.

Poitier, Sidney. *This Life*. New York: Alfred A. Knopf, 1980.

Pounds, Michael Charles. "Details in Black: A Case Study Investigation and Analysis of the Content of the United States War Department Non-Fiction Motion Picture *The Negro Soldier*." Diss., New York University, 1981.

Reid, Mark Allen. "The 1949 Problem Film: An Analysis of Hollywood's Treatment of Racism." Thesis, University of Illinois at Chicago Circle, 1979.

———. "Med Hondo Interview: Working Abroad." *Jump Cut* 31 (March 1986): 48–49.

———. "Early Black Independent Filmmakers." *Black Film Review* 2 (Fall 1986): 21–22.

———. "Two Black French Filmmakers." *Black Film Review* 3 (Winter 1986–1987): 8–12.

———. "Dialogic Modes of Representing Africa(s): Womanist Film." *Black American Literature Forum* 25 (Summer 1991): 375–388.

———. "The U.S. Black Family Film." *Jump Cut* 36 (1991): 81–88.

Robinson, Louie. "Michael Schultz: A Rising Star Behind the Camera." *Ebony* (September 1978): 94–96, 98, 100, 102.

Roffman, Peter, and Bev Simpson. "Black Images on White Screens." *Cineaste* 13 (June 1984): 14–21.

Rovin, Jeff. *Richard Pryor Black and Blue.* New York: Bantam Books, 1984.

Schatz, Thomas. *Hollywood Genres: Formulas, Filmmaking, and the Studio System.* Philadelphia: Temple University Press, 1981.

———. *Old Hollywood/New Hollywood: Ritual, Art, and Industry.* Ann Arbor: UMI Research Press, 1983.

Schultz, Michael. Personal interview with the author. 28 July 1987.

Shankman, Arnold. "Black Pride and Protest: The Amos 'N' Andy Crusade." *Journal of Popular Culture* 12 (Fall 1979): 236–252.

Sharpe, Robert K. Letter to David Susskind. 21 March 1961. David Susskind Papers, Wisconsin State Historical Society, Madison, Wisconsin.

Smith, Ronald Lande. *Cosby.* New York: St. Martin's Press, 1986.

———. *The Stars of Stand-up Comedy.* New York: Garland Publishing, 1986.

Stam, Robert, and Louise Spence. "Colonialism, Racism, and Representation: An Introduction." In Vol. 2, *Movies and Methods.* Ed. Bill Nichols. Berkeley, Los Angeles, London: University of California Press, 1985.

Steinberg, Cobbett. *Reel Facts: The Movie Books of Records.* New York: Vintage Books, 1982.

Stern, Harold. Letter to Bernard Birnbaum. 1 June 1960. David Susskind Papers, Wisconsin State Historical Society, Madison, Wisconsin.

Susskind, David. Letter to Sam Briskin. 13 March 1959. David Susskind Papers, Wisconsin State Historical Society, Madison, Wisconsin.

Taylor, Clyde. "Visionary Black Cinema." *The Black Collegian* (October–November 1980): 34–35.

———. "Black Films in Search of a Home." *Freedomways* 23, no. 4 (1983): 226–233.

Terrace, Vincent. *The Complete Encyclopedia of Television Series, Plots and Specials, 1937–1973.* Vol. 1. New York: Zoetrope, 1986.

Turner, Darwin T. "Dramas of Black Life from 1953–1970." *Iowa Review* 6, no. 2 (Spring 1975): 82–99.

Van Peebles, Melvin. *The Making of Sweet Sweetback's Baadasssss Song.* New York: Lancer Books, 1972.

Watkins, Mel. "Writing in Black and White." *Chamba Notes* (Summer 1980): 9–10.

Welker, Robert H. "New Image of American Black." *Variety* (1 Feb. 1961): 7, 19.

West, Hollie. "Black Films: Crossovers and Beyond Blaxploitation." *Washington Post,* 8 Feb. 1976.

Williams, Christopher, ed. "Forms and Ideologies." In *Realism and the Cinema: A Reader.* London: Routledge and Kegan Paul, 1980.

Williams, Robert F. "From Negroes with Guns." In *Black On Black: Commentaries by Negro Americans.* Ed. Arnold Adoff. Toronto, Canada: Macmillan Company, 1969.

Wollen, Peter. "Godard and Counter Cinema: Vent d'Est." In *Readings and Writings: Semiotic Counter-Strategies.* London: Verso Editions and NLB, 1982.

Wright, Richard. "Introduction: Blueprint for Negro Writing." In *The Black Aesthetic*. Ed. Addison Gayle, Jr. Garden City, N.Y.: Doubleday and Company, 1972.

Yearwood, Gladstone L., ed. *Black Cinema Aesthetics: Issues in Independent Black Filmmaking*. Athens, Ohio: Ohio University Center for Afro-American Studies, 1982.

Zeutlin, Barbara, and David Talbot. *Creative Differences: Profiles of Hollywood Dissidents*. Boston: South End Press, 1978.

Index

Index of Film Titles

Designer: U.C. Press Staff
Compositor: Huron Valley Graphics
Text: 10/12 Times Roman
Display: Times Roman
Printer: Haddon Craftsmen Inc.
Binder: Haddon Craftsmen Inc.